GOLF BEGINS AT FORTY

GOLF BEGINS AT FORTY

Earl Stewart, Jr., and Dr. Harry E. (Bud) Gunn

Greatlakes Living Press, Publishers, Matteson, Illinois

Golf Begins At Forty
© Earl Stewart, Jr. and Dr. Harry E. (Bud) Gunn 1977
All rights reserved
Printed in U.S.A.
Library of Congress Catalog Card No.: 77-71556
International Standard Book Number: 0-915498-45-6

Cover design by Paul J. Henderson / St. Louis
Photography by Patrick K. Snook

Greatlakes Living Press
21750 Main Street
Matteson, Illinois 60443

Contents

Foreword

Having known Earl Stewart, Jr. for the majority of my golfing life, I know of no one who has devoted more conscientious effort to the great game of golf. His background as an outstanding junior player, an excellent amateur, a tournament winner on the professional golf tour, a great club professional, a teacher, a golf coach, and now, being over 40 years old qualifies him to be the author of this book.

Once a player has broken the 40 barrier, there are certain changes in his golf game that are mandatory. Some come naturally, others take a few "smarts," some practice and effort. I, myself, have had to change my mental approach to the game, concentrating on finesse and consistency, rather than power and force.

I wholeheartedly recommend Earl Stewart as an instructor of older players, because he understands so well the change of attitude necessary for a better golf game after the age of 40.

Don January

Introduction

U. S. Census figures show that a larger percentage of our population lives longer than ever before. The number of persons in the middle to older age bracket has increased as a result of better nutrition and more advanced medical care. At the same time, modern technology has provided us with more leisure time and lessened the amount of hard physical labor that must be done when we are working.

With more time on their hands, what will all these older people do? Few of us have had much preparation for more joyful and constructive use of leisure time. We work hard to get to the retired years and then find ourselves bored. Doctors tell us to remain active, and yet most of us participate in sports that can't be enjoyed much past 35. At that age, for example, the professional player—in football, baseball, basketball, and hockey—is considered old. By 40 these athletes are out of their professions. How do *they* stay active?

Most people do not want merely to expend energy. If they spend time at a sport, they want to enjoy that sport's physical activity by developing some proficiency in it. Few of us enjoy what we can't do with at least a fair degree of skill.

Yet almost every sport demands physical prowess that a person past his physical prime no longer possesses. In addition, developing a skill in most sports must begin when the player is rather young. Swimming, for example, is an excellent sport for the older person. But it is exceedingly difficult to be a strong swimmer without having developed lung capacity and muscle strength at a young age. I will provide some evidence to suggest that this is not the case with golf.

The game of golf also provides many other advantages that are worthy of mention. Human beings are gregarious and golf is the type of game that lends itself to social contact. At the same time all of us have occasions when we wish to be alone. Golf meets that need, too, since it can be played alone. In most sports, we find ourselves out of place if we participate with others whose skills differ widely from our own. In tennis, for example, a pleasant game means that opponents must be relatively evenly matched with each other. If one of the tennis players can't even return the shots hit by his opponent, what pleasure can either one of them get from their game? In golf, the situation is different. As long as one player does not hold up his fellow golfers, it won't matter what sort of score he makes. I have seen many players shoot 100 and yet play as rapidly as the low handicapper. It is true, therefore, that golfers with different levels of ability can play very compatibly together, while this is generally not the case in other sports.

Importantly related to this point is the ability of golfers with different levels of skill to compete against each other on an even basis. Most persons have competitive needs that push for expression. Athletics can serve as an excellent outlet for this need. Again, however, the nature of most sports prevents players at different levels of skill from being able to compete evenly with one another. They would either get hurt physically or there would be no contest. The handicap system in golf, on the other hand, provides an equitable means of comparing golf performances.

Golf as a sport has numerous other advantages for the older person. It is not a game that produces a large number of injuries. A businessman does not run the risk of damaging his body to the extent that his business career will be temporarily halted. A person does not have to be in such perfect physical condition that he must dramatically alter his life style in order to participate. In fact, people play golf after recuperating from heart attacks and other illness. Many individuals who are missing a limb play a strong game. If a person maintains reasonable health, he can continue to play golf virtually all his life. Even those who have trouble walking can now play by using electric carts. The physical surroundings in golf—trees, ponds, brooks, grassy knolls, and the clean, sunny outdoors—are among the most pleasant and healthiest in athletics.

The social aspect of the game is important, too. An entire family can play the sport together, for example. Indeed, there are few other sports that a grandfather and grandmother can play with their grandchildren. Good friendships often develop on the golf course. In addition, the social aspect of the game blends easily into a healthy business relationship. The time between shots, for example, lends itself to relaxed conversation about business matters. This is one reason why many of our large companies maintain country club affiliation for their key employees.

My point is that while the game of golf has numerous advantages for just about anyone, it has even more advantages for the older person. Yet there is little available on the instructional market for the older player. Literally hundreds of golf books have been written, generally by tour or former tour players. What works for the man who is young, strong, and playing everyday is not likely to work, however, for the older person. Adjustments and adaptations simply must be made by the older person who plays golf, just as what proves successful for the tour professional will not be likely to work for the average to high handicapper.

The major tenet of this book, then, is that golf life does not end at age 40. But the golfer or potential golfer must be realistic: What works for the 20 year old is not likely to work for the older player. The same is true in terms of beginning the game at an older age. If you have never played golf before age 40, your method of learning will be notably dissimilar to that of the beginning teenager. Life is a matter of adaptations, and so is golf. The purpose of this book is to provide an instructional manual for the older person. It is designed for those who wish to improve their games and also for those who wish to begin the game after age 40. I believe that either of those desires can be satisfied by a solid application of the material in this book.

*To our wives, Dot Stewart and Vi Gunn,
who have made life after 40
better than ever.*

Over-40 models, from left to right: Pat Martin, Earl Stewart, Marge Fiegel.

1

Is It Ever Too Late to Play Golf?

Make golf a part of your life, with positive thoughts, age-oriented goals and guidance from the over-40 pros.

I am tempted to answer this question with an emphatic *never,* but, on the other hand, some qualification is in order. The most important qualification concerns the goals of the individual. When a person talks about playing the game, does he mean playing well enough to make it around the course before dark? Or does he mean being able to break 100? Or is he referring to scoring near par figures and perhaps even becoming a champion? We need to know what degree of proficiency a golfer seeks.

First of all, some basic skills are needed in order to enjoy the game of golf. The game is just not much fun for a golfer or his playing partners if he is constantly searching for errant balls. Nor is it enjoyable to take a swipe at the ball and completely miss it. The main thing needed to enjoy the game is an ability to advance the ball consistently and *generally* keep it in play. I say *generally* because none of us can keep it in play all of the time. You do not have to play golf in near par figures in order to find pleasure. You can set up your own par, for example, and shoot at that. If you can generally keep the ball in play and hit it close to 150 yards, you can play with anyone. And if in addition you can sharpen your short game you would have a good chance of playing better than bogey golf, or less than one over par per hole.

The effects of a golfer's age on these goals must naturally be taken into account. I have strong feelings about those effects, because I believe our society tends to be too negative about age. We often read articles that suggest that a person in his fifties is nearly useless. Many seem to believe that our bodies nearly fall apart when we reach sixty, if not before that. This line of thought, if believed, can cause a more rapid aging process and even a type of withdrawal. When people feel useless they avoid not only physical activities but also social functions. They may even retire early because they feel they can't contribute. To me, however, being old is feeling old.

I have great admiration for performers such as George Burns, who goes right on dancing and making appearances at an advanced age. Or look at the active life in public affairs Israel's Golda Meir has led. We talk about the loss of nerve control and dexterity age supposedly brings, yet look at the number of highly skilled surgeons who continue to practice late in life. How could they continue to operate and save people's lives if their nerves really began to fail at age 40? Consequently, I firmly believe that age alone is not a serious obstacle to anyone who wishes to play golf all his life. Golf is a game for an entire lifetime, and the growing number of older people playing it proves this. Modern medicine is helping people to not only live longer but also to stay relatively healthy later in life. Perhaps it is time that we developed a modern psychology adapted to our modern medical achievements.

The prospects for an older person who wishes to play a highly skilled game of golf, as distinct from an ordinary game, a more difficult question to answer because it involves many different factors. How much time, energy, and drive does that person possess? Developing a strong golf game takes practice and dedication, irrespective of age. An older person, however, often finds heavy demands placed upon his time. Family, occupation, perhaps civic responsibilities all take their toll—and that's as it should be for a person who wishes to lead a full life. The younger person usually has fewer demands placed upon his time, and he can therefore devote more time to each activity. This is not to say that with age we necessarily have less time for golf. We may be able to balance our lives so that we have the opportunity for regular physical activities along with our other pursuits. A person can develop a very sound golf game without spending great quantities of time on the golf course. In that case, he simply has to get the most out of the time available.

The rest of a golfer's lifestyle, then, probably affects his game more than his age. This means that an older player must ask himself how much golf time his lifestyle will allow. What are his other priorities? How much time, energy, and devotion can be made available for golf?

The effect of age itself on a golfer's ability is universal. If the desire is there, an older golfer can accomplish a great deal. Age does affect golfing ability, but it does not automatically handicap it. There is much evidence available that supports this statement. Let's look at the accomplishments of some of the older players.

In the amateur ranks, Dale Morey has made strong showings in national tournaments in recent years. Bill Hyndman won a national tournament and was medalist in a recent Transmississippi Amateur. Bill's is a great achievement for anyone, and he is close to sixty. These two men have been able to stay on top of their professions while still maintaining very strong golf games. That proves that neither age nor business demands can make championship-caliber amateur golf impossible.

Nor does age alone prevent championship golf in the professional rands. Julius Borus, Ben Hogan, Sam Snead and Art Wall have continued to play well right through their older years. In 1976, Don January had a particularly outstanding year. He recently won the Professional Golfers' Association national tournament, and thereby qualified for the Tournament of Champions. He went on to win the latter event in 1976 and in that same year won more than $160,000. Don has been an excellent player for many years, and it would seem that he has lost very little golfing ability at age 46.

Don recently wrote me a letter talking about the effects of age on his golf game. In that letter he says:

"Once a player breaks the 40 barrier, certain changes in his game become mandatory. Some come naturally; others take a good deal of thinking, practice, and effort to master. As for myself, I have changed to a softer, or weaker, shaft, and less weight in the clubhead. These changes give me more clubhead speed, compensating for distance lost as a result of not being as strong as I once was. I have had to change my mental approach to the game, concentrating less on power and force and more on finesse and consistency. The most important change I have made, and the hardest to accomplish, has been becoming aware that my nerves are now a negative factor to my game and that I must reverse control and channel them towards positive results."

The changes that Don has made are consistent with advice given in other chapters in this book. What especially impresses me is Don's idea of changing negative thoughts to positive ones. I advocate that for all of my students, regardless of age. But it is particularly necessary for the older player, and it can be done. Don January is an excellent example because in 1976 he won $163,622 and the Vardon Trophy for that year. The latter goes to the player with the lowest scoring average on the professional tour and who has played at least 80 rounds of golf. The requirement of so many rounds means that the winner of this coveted award must be extremely consistent.

These experiences of amateurs and professional golfers should offer great encouragement to all older people who wish to take up golf. This is a great game for everyone, and older people have no good reason to feel they can't hold their own on the course.

So to those who ask, "When do you get too old for golf?," I reply that you never do until such a time as you *feel* too old. Think young, keep your health up and you can be a good golfer—possibly even of championship caliber. I also firmly believe that successfully competing on the golf course develops a mental attitude that positively reinforces everything else a person does in life.

2

How to Develop a Better Mental Attitude

Build a winning attitude, by perfecting your touch and finesse, learning to relax, accepting physical limitations and setting your own pace.

It is unlikely that anyone can become consistently successful in any sport unless he develops a good mental attitude. As we watch sporting contests on television we constantly hear phrases such as "this team is really up," or "this coach knows how to motivate his players," or "this team can't win because they seem down." All of these comments reflect what has been called the *winning attitude.* It is an ill-defined aspect of athletics, and yet everyone recognizes the vital role that emotions play in even the most physical of games.

While successful competition in just about any sport requires a winning attitude, that attitude is doubly necessary in golf. Most experts agree that golf is a truly mental game. It has been estimated that about 80 percent of a golfer's success is attributable to psychological factors. That is one of the reasons why psychologists find this game so fascinating. The mental aspect outweighs the physical part of the game, and success or failure generally hinges on the mental attitude. The game of golf seems to bring out, sooner or later, every latent personality trait. I firmly believe that a good study of an individual's personality could be made merely by observing him a few times on the golf course.

There are any number of reasons why psychology and golf are so inherently linked together. Whereas many other sports are fast reflex games, golf is a slow game that requires thoughtful study. When a baseball is pitched at nearly 100 miles an hour, the batter can't do much more than react. There simply is no time for real thinking. And if the batter hits a foul ball out of play, he gets another pitch, with a new ball, and another chance in the batter's box. He doesn't have to hunt the foul ball up and develop a plan to get it back in play again. I am not claiming baseball or any other sport involves no intelligent thinking. They certainly do, but generally that thinking takes place either before or after—and not during—the heat of the action.

The point is that golf requires and facilitates constant thought during the game. Club selection is an example. Since there are 14 clubs in a set, the player must make basic decisions about which one to use at nearly every shot. Should he use a three wood off the tee to stay short of those fairway bunkers, or should he use his driver and try to clear them? Should he play a wedge shot straight to the pin, or hit a low shot and stay under the wind? Would a chip out of the sand be safer, or is it advisable to hit a long explosion type of shot? These are just a few of the kinds of decisions that must be made in each round. Golfing provides time to think, and, being human, we enjoy that highly challenging part of the game.

The slowness of the game also facilitates more self analysis that is found in nearly any other sport. Golfers can remember their shots for a very long time, with the resulting tendency to think about what "went wrong" or "what they did right" on that shot. There is a lot of opportunity to be alone on a golf course, even when playing in a foursome, and the time between shots provides plenty of opportunity for analysis. This is why golfers generally analyze their own performances, both mental and physical, more constantly than do other athletes.

Success or failure is directly related to what the individual player does, so it is easy to pinpoint his performance. There is not a backup person to save you if you blow a shot. The golfer makes every shot, and he does it by himself. He may offer bad luck as an alibi, but in the final analysis all results depend on him.

Finally, golf is a game where touch and finesse are exceedingly important. A player can drive a ball 300 yards only to nullify that achievement if he loses his touch with his wedge or putter. The fine muscles are involved with touch, and they are intricately tied into the central nervous system. This means that any negative thoughts or doubts will inevitably disrupt the muscular functioning that controls the player's touch. His game will become jerky and erratic. It is axiomatic, therefore, that in order to play well a golfer must develop a certain amount of self mastery through a sound psychological approach to the game.

What is especially interesting to me as a psychologist in this context is the fact that what is learned in one endeavor can be used in other areas. We call this "the transfer of learning," and pertinent to this chapter it means that what is learned on the golf course can apply to our lives in general. If we can learn how to develop a winning attitude on the golf course, we have learned tactics that can help make our whole lives happier and easier. We can help reduce the mental handicap that plagues most of us in many of the things we do.

Let me give you an illustration. More than 30 years ago I knew a fellow golfer at Olympia Fields Country Club who had an excellent golf swing. He took lessons by the dozens, spent many hours on the practice tee and had a very low handicap. Yet, try as he might, he could never win the club championship. In fact he never even got to the finals! It was comon gossip around the club that he "psyched himself," and thereby was a consistent loser.

He always defended himself by ridiculing those comments, but he was never able to improve his competitive record. One year, John had a great game going and yet he still lost in the very opening round of the championship. To make matters worse he was beaten by a man whose handicap was nine shots higher.

John was understandably perplexed by his ignominious defeat and he sought my counsel as a psychologist. His major question was whether I felt he repeatedly "psyched" himself into losing. I answered that I wasn't sure but that perhaps I could offer an opinion if I knew more about the remainder of his life. That question stimulated a lengthy conversation that underlined business failures in abundance. John earned a fairly good income but nothing like that which was achieved by others in similar positions. At one point he even mentioned he often lost sales that were supposed to be "sure things," only to make a sale where it was deemed most unlikely.

We next talked about John's marriage, which perhaps could be summarized by saying that John and his wife never seemed able to tolerate a good time. They both came to fear those periods when things were going well because they were sure to have some "irrational fight over literally nothing."

I listened carefully for nearly an hour and then suggested to John that there was some evidence he was a self-defeating person. I told him I had no idea how or why this happened but explained it is fairly common. When he asked me how he could find the probable cause of his apparently self-deafeating attitude, I suggested as one possibility that he see a therapist. I explained no one was suggesting he was a sick person but rather that there might be a hidden problem.

John decided to think it over but several months later he called me again. He had suffered a business setback and wanted to take a closer look at his personality. I referred him to a colleague of mine and he began the process of self-understanding. During the winter John was transferred to another area and at Christmas I received a card saying he was continuing his program with another psychologist.

I did not see or hear from John for another year, and then one day he unexpectedly dropped by the country club. I was sitting alone having lunch when he asked to join me. We were chatting away about little things when John finally smiled and said, "Would you believe I won my club championship last year?"

With that statement I took a closer look at John. He did seem different: more confident, relaxed, and able to laugh and joke around. I couldn't resist the question—"What changed?"

John went on to say that what started as an attempt to discover why he failed on the golf course ended with discovery about his whole life. The crux of the matter had been his relationship with his father. In many ways his father was a very good father; warm, involved, generally easy to talk to, and proud of his son. In fact, father and son had done many things together from the time John was an infant. The father had married late in life and nearly given up hope of ever having a son. When John was born his father was beside himself with joy. He had great expectations for his son and was a constant companion and teacher.

The relationship was generally excellent and the son had a strong desire to please his father because of the latter's warmth, support and general emotional investment. John stated that his father literally "felt I could do anything."

It was there that the rub began to develop. John's father was a believer in steady and consistent improvement. He constantly taught that the human mind and body can always put out a little extra. If you run the 100 yard dash in 11 seconds today, then tomorrow you can put out a little more effort and cut your time to 10.9 seconds.

John began to fear letting his father down. The expectations were becoming too high and the constant pressure to improve took a very heavy toll. "Where does it all stop?" John found himself wondering, "If I give my best today," he came to realize, "I am in real trouble tomorrow." Today's successes became the yardstick to judge the next day's performance. But if he did not do his best today then there was not so great pressure the next time. John finally concluded that had he won the club championship he literally would have had no place to go but up. By not becoming a winner he was guarding himself against future dramatic failures. Achievement in the future was open because it had not yet taken place.

John verified some of these ideas by stating he always feared any performance that could not be topped. If he received 100 in a school spelling test, for example, there was no place to go but down.

What seemed especially important to me about the self-discovery John had made was not only its carryover to the golf course, but its carryover to other parts of his life. His marriage improved and so did his ability to earn a living. He has won his club championship five times now, and the rest of his life also continues to improve.

Building a winning attitude on the golf course furnishes ideas that help elsewhere too. This is particularly true since we are seeking to build a better mental attitude for the older player, and many of the problems of the older person are psychological. This brings us to an important discussion that we might call *the psychology of aging.* Let's look at what happens with age.

There is ample evidence these days that what happens to older people is generally what they expect to happen. Negative thinking again, but in this case it seems more caused by the attitudes of society than initially by the individual himself. People have been told that they must retire at a specific age because they won't be able to handle their jobs past that point. The suggestion is made that they slow down because otherwise they might precipitate a heart attack or do some other kind of bodily harm to themselves. We have long believed that sexual functioning ceases past 55 or 60 years old. We often act as though we have to struggle to find some activity whose only function is to people *occupied* in their later years.

How ironic this is when the same society that conveys those messages, and worships youth, nearly always selects for its leaders older men. It is rare for a presidential candidate to be younger than 55. Even if he is under 55, he probably will be over that age by the time he finishes his first term. Supreme Court justices are always older, as are most generals and presidents of large companies.

A number of recent studies have come along that demonstrate the fallacy of our earlier thinking. Even in our sexual lives, we have been deceived. It seems that people well into old age (80s and 90s) can sexually perform very well as long as they are healthy, happily married, and self confident.

Just recently, too, a British doctor has announced that years of study have convinced him that the brain does not shrink with age (as has been thought), and that there is no loss of IQ and no significant loss of memory. What does happen is that the memory slows down. The good doctor did find some loss of reflex speed, and it's always been generally known that aging causes loss of strength. Most significantly, though, the study showed that the biggest loss agaimg causes is in self-esteem. This seems to happen because so many segments of modern society take negative pot shots at the older person.

In my own practice I have seen examples of this. Older persons come to me with feelings of depression that have arisen from feelings of unworthiness. These people often do not know what to do with themselves because they are deemdd too old to work and they know they can't play as they did when they were younger. In many cases the depression melts away when they are helped to find activities that allow them to be productive and useful. They are happy to find they have not suffered a loss of mental ability, and in most cases they are able to do more physical work than they realized. I am a great believer in physical activity as a guard against mental unbalance. I think the ancient Greeks were correct when they said, "healthy body, healthy mind." It has always been interesting to me to note how few breakdowns there are among highly athletic people.

These professional observations of mine suggest the importance of the correct mental attitude—and they show that people do not need to fall apart because of older age. Most deterioration that does accompany the aging process can be traced to a faulty mental attitude. Let's take a look at those steps that will help us build up a positive mental attitude.

First, in order to conquer negative thinking it helps to know what you are up against. So let us accept the fact that our society preaches that as people grow older they become scatter-brained and suffer other deterioration. I have presented evidence that contradicts that belief, but it is not easy to overcome what is constantly hammered into us. Along with understanding what he's up against, therefore, an older person should ask himself whether he *sees* any actual deterioration or whether he simply accepts it without confirming evidence. Chances are the person uncritically believes what he has been told.

Secondly, it is always easier for people to make excuses for their failures rather than to accept some personal shortcoming. How many times have you heard one person say that he could play as well as another if only he had the time to practice? But would he work on his game if he did have the time? Probably not, because generally if he'd had the desire he would have found a way. Age itself can be an excuse. It lets a person off the hook because there is nothing he can do about his age. So the second way to develop a winning attitude is to stop complaining and making excuses and to take a good look at ourselves, identifying weaknesses and taking steps to correct them.

The third way an older person develops a winning attitude is by accepting the fact that he is going to have negative thoughts at times. This happens to anyone, however, regardless of age. So what the older person needs to do is what anyone else needs to do: cut down the number and frequency of negative thoughts, while at the same time accepting the fact that some are bound to occur. There is a negative part in everyone's life, because nobody's life goes exactly as he desires. People commonly have depressions, discouragements and anxieties. If we could only come to realize that these, too, are part of life perhaps these distresses wouldn't seem so grave. When something blocks what we'd like to do, we might tell ourselves that this, too, will pass away— and it almost always will. This is the first step in reducing shock and turning a negative thought into a positive thought. We can try harder, concentrate more completely and fight back. Life then becomes a challenge as far as overcoming the defeatist part of ourselves. In golf, for example, when nagging self-doubt attacks a player he can fight back by concentrating on swing basics and thereby occupy his mind with something constructive. It is important to remember that most of us can concentrate only on one thing at a time. If we think of what we want to do and how to do it we will not have time for negative thinking.

One of the most devastating negative thoughts, and one that's particularly important for a person to overcome, is the expectation that something is about to go seriously wrong. I have seen many players who normally shoot around 100 start off with a 40 on the front nine. Then they start telling themselves that their games will have to fall apart on the back nine because they are playing way over their heads. They literally *expect* to shoot 60 on the back nine. So they tense up, forcing the golf swing to fall apart. A golfer in this position should instead approach the back nine with the idea that he's really got something going for himself today. He's either learned something new or made some improvements. If 40 has been his best 9-hole score ever, he may not equal it again—but he certainly should be able to play within 10 strokes of it. That attitude builds confidence. It relaxes a person and enables him to keep improving. And let me mention one related word of caution. Many people subconsciously become jealous of someone else who shows more rapid improvement than they do. Someone's front-nine score of 40, for example, will cause them to make negative comments about what will likely happen on the back nine. If these remarks should happen to come your way, let them roll off your back. Think to yourself that these people are talking about *their* experiences, not *yours.*

A fourth means of developing the winning attitude involves improving the way we see ourselves. Psychologists have always taken interest in the self-concept aspect of the human personality. This one aspect tells a great deal about the functioning of an individual, answering such questions as: Is he confident of himself? Does he give up easily? How does he react to pressure? Does he block himself from learning new activities?

The concept of oneself involves an inner feeling about the self that is not totally influenced by what currently happens. That feeling includes a long residue of similar past feelings. People who are very insecure do not suddenly become secure when they do something well. Doing something well can for a short time make them feel less insecure, but at the first slight hint of failure their confidence crumbles. They need constant reassurance, and life seldom affords that. After all, every person and every golfer experiences failure. The greatest golfer in the world doesn't always win, and he doesn't always match or break par. The insecure person tends to set impossible goals for himself, so he seldom knows the satisfaction of a job well done.

I want to make a very important distinction at this point. I am not suggesting that anyone stop striving for continual improvement. Growth and development are definitely important. I am against the idea, however, that a person must keep getting closer and closer to perfection in order to feel *adequate.* In psychological terms, striving to improve represents "ego expansion," or the development of the self; while being unsatisfied with anything else than perfection represents the use of an "ego crutch." If you always have to prove something to yourself or to others, you will never be a relaxed, confident person and life will be one battle after another. And you will never develop a winning attitude. If you play any kind of competitive golf you will fall apart as soon as you hit a few bad shots. Anger and self-recrimination will replace confidence and reason.

I believe that golf can provide a vehicle towards better self-understanding and personality growth. It is the kind of game that puts the personality on display. It might be a good idea after a round of golf to think back over what you did on the course. Here are some key things to look for. Do you become angry every time you hit a poor shot? Are you under constant pressure out there? Do you find that you are seldom satisfied with anything you do? Do you pout after a bad shot and tend to become withdrawn? In other words, does golf become a life-or-death proposition?

If you are answering *yes* to many of these questions you should consider why you are playing the game. Golf is a game for enjoyment and the pleasure of intelligently executed physical expression. It is a game that places one challenge after another in front of you. So does life, and humans are created to enjoy that. But since no one likes a challenge that can never be met, be careful not to place too much of a burden upon yourself.

I am talking here of the establishment of goals that are reasonable. It can simply be stated as a sound psychological principle that when we place too much pressure upon ourselves there is something very wrong. We are trying to bolster a sagging self concept. We are then *using* golf (or business), or whatever, as a crutch—and the crutch won't work.

You can attack that problem in two ways. The most difficult one is to try to examine yourself (while off the course) to try to locate those factors that have caused the basic insecurity. In the example of my friend John it was his relationship with his father. Generally when you find the cause or causes you will be able to remove the nagging self-doubt.

Secondly, with the game of golf itself, learn to set realistic goals. You will never hit every shot perfectly. Neither will Jack Nicklaus, and if he can accept that fact, why can't you? You may decide to set up your own par figures. If you generally shoot 100, then why not set par figure as a bogey per hole? That would give you a score of 90 if you shoot to your par. And 90 is the sort of game that will allow you to play with anyone, because it means you are losing only one shot per hole to actual par for the course.

Mis-hit shots are also part of the game. If you watch the professionals you will see that they fall well short of hitting every green in regulation figures. In fact, if they hit 12 of 18 greens in those figures, they are performing above average. The important thing is to accept the errant shot as another challenge that the game provides. And this acceptance of less-than-perfect shots as inevitable and challenging usually enables a golfer to relax and do better.

Golf can provide another valuable lesson for life as a whole. Each person over the course of any given day is likely to feel angry, frustrated, tense, and anxious along with the more joyful emotions. That is entirely normal, as any psychologist will verify. What really counts is the way a person handles these emotions. There are two extremes that are harmful. One is to hold in the anger, or other intense emotion, and seldom or never show it. This builds up to periodic explosions, however, or else makes a person constantly tense. The other extreme is the constant emotional explosion, such as throwing clubs or ranting and raving. Both extremes are harmful to life and the game of golf. Learn to handle your emotions on the course by accepting them, giving them verbal ventilation and thus reducing them. The simple remark, "Oh damn, that makes me angry," will go far towards tension reduction. You can even say it to yourself if need be.

Older people have an advantage here, because they generally exercise more self-control and patience than do younger people. They have had to develop those qualities over the years in order to handle life. And they can use those same qualities on the golf course to release pent-up tensions in a controlled manner.

There is another advantage that comes with age, and it too can be put to excellent use on the course. Youth is impulsive; age adds wisdom and thoughtfulness. Since golf is a thinking man's game you can improve your performance by planning. Develop a strategy that fits your level of skill. Earl Stewart has always told me to stick with shots that I have a good chance of making. Plan those tee shots, for example, so you have a shot to the green. Don't try to pull off a one-in-a-million shot that probably will get you into serious difficulty. Don't over-analyze your swing or yourself but stick with whatever usually works well.

Earl makes another point in his teaching that is very sound psychologically. Avoid over-thinking. Learn the basics of the swing and then concentrate only on the central ideas. This helps improve concentration because it cuts down what a person has to think about. The mind remains free and uncluttered. I have seen many players become aggravated because on a particular day they are fading the ball. Perhaps they usually hook the same shots. So they start to tear apart the whole swing to find the error. Earl's idea of going with the shot they have that day makes sense. It keeps you with the basic idea that you need not hit perfect shots to score well. So you play that fade and capitalize on what you have going for you. You don't try to force the swing into a preconceived mold.

One final bit of advice can help improve your mental attitude. It comes under the heading of doing your own thing. I have heard many stories about how one person tries to "psych" another and thereby win some competitive contest. Studies done with professional athletes indicate this seldom takes place. Those who are successful concentrate on their own performance and not upon what someone else does.

I think you can learn from these studies and apply the resultant knowledge to your golf game even if you don't wish to play competitively. Golfers are notorious for watching each other and then trying to make imitations. Earl Stewart long ago proved to me that I can't swing like Arnold Palmer. What works for him wouldn't for me. Yet I have seen older players struggle to try to keep up with younger players off the tee. In so doing they succeeded only in destroying the accuracy and finesse in their own games. They lost all consistency and were soon convinced that they were "too old to play this game."

One of the marvelous characteristics of golf is that you *do* get to do your own thing. No one else can do anything to you; only you can do it to yourself. You don't have to play like anyone else and you should not try. Learn to stay with what works for you and never lament what you can't do. Fight a personal battle to develop your own strengths and you can become a winner.

Above all remember that *feeling* old is *being* old. Turn negative attitudes into positive thoughts. Don't complain about lost strength; concentrate instead on the greater wisdom, patience and self-control that age brings. Learning to think positively on the golf course gets you past the first and biggest challenge out there, and puts you in a position to master the physical aspects of the game that Earl Stewart presents in the following chapters.

3

The Grip:
Vital Link to the Club

Compensate for loss of power and increase comfort, consistency and control in your grip, by balancing your hands, avoiding the strong grip and doing what feels best for YOU.

The importance of the grip to a sound golf game can't be overemphasized. After all, the grip is precisely what connects the player and his club. When I speak of this phrase of the game for the older player, I certainly am not implying the younger player doesn't need to concentrate on a proper grip. *All* players must do it.

However, because an older player is bound to lose some of his physical strength, he can no longer even partially compensate for a poor swing with brute force. In order to make up for some loss of power and strength, he must develop better rhythm and better feel, or touch. And it's impossible for anyone to improve his touch without a proper grip.

To begin with the general principles that apply to anyone's golf swing, we can say that the swing consists of a number of different parts that are all molded together into a unit. Every phase of a good swing is tied together, or synchronized. Now obviously, a person in the midst of a swing can't be thinking about each of its parts as he goes along without destroying the unity of the swing. The goal must be to make the swing automatic; that is, to reduce conscious thought about its various elements during the swing. All of these elements work and move together in synchronization only when the swing begins properly. This starting point for the swing, which golfers refer to as the *set-up,* is the key to everything that follows. I believe it causes all elements in the swing to synchronize with each other, thus producing consistently good golf shots. Starting with a proper set-up reduces the really vast number of errors that can ruin a golf swing. A poor set-up, on the other hand, greatly increases the likelihood of those errors happening. And since the first action a golfer takes in setting himself up is gripping the club, everything else in the swing starts with that grip. I have seen many swings ruined from the very start because the golfer had a faulty grip on his club.

A good grip must be comfortable and secure. If it's too tight, the player's muscles tend to lock and, in turn, impede backswing motion with the club. If the grip is too loose, by contrast, the player is apt to lose full control of the club somewhere in the backswing, probably causing a very loose or flippy type of swing. The question, therefore, is how tightly to grip a golf club without that grip being either too tight or too loose. And indeed there is no absolute answer to the question, no one rule that applies to everyone. About all that I or anybody else can say is to avoid the extremes of tightness and looseness, for reasons already given, but at the same time to have a secure enough hold on the club to control it throughout the swing. The grip should also be uniform throughout the swing, not tightened at one point and relaxed at another. Each golfer needs to experiment to find where his grip is firm enough to give control and yet relaxed enough to prevent the muscles from locking. If he finds that his grip is slightly firmer or looser than that of another player, he needn't worry that he's wrong. What he does need to watch out for is the tendency of the slightly firmer grip toward strangulation and that of the slightly looser grip toward sloppiness.

Then there is the question about the *type* of grip to use. People often talk about *strong* and *weak* grips, by which they distinguish different placements of the right hand. When the right hand goes under the grip (or to the golfer's right), this is considered, in the game's terminology, a strong grip. When the right hand moves more to the top of the grip, this is normally considered a weaker right hand grip. However, again, I want to state that it is my belief that not every individual will have the same sort of grip. There is a good deal of variation even among fine professional players. Ten different players will quite likely place their hands in 10 different positions. Consequently, I will talk about grip variations and will leave it to the individual golfer to select that grip which works most effectively for him. Remember, the best results in golf come from fitting the game to the individual and not forcing each individaul into one theoretical mold. That's why I don't believe there's one perfect way to play golf, and that's why I don't believe there's only one proper way to grip a club. I will describe the three most commonly used—the Vardon grip, the interlocking grip and the baseball grip—but choosing between these variations finally is up to each player. How does he make the choice? By determining which one consistently produces the best results for him, and with the greatest comfort.

Once a player finds the grip that meets these standards, and after enough experimentation, he should stick with it even if other golfers call the grip "unorthodox." I recall the experience of Vi Gunn, my co-author's wife, in this regard. She had been using the interlocking grip, and I never saw her lose control of the club. A year later·she could barely hold onto it, and when I checked her grip I noticed that she was no longer employing her former grip. Someone had told her it was a faulty grip, and unfortunately she had changed. Once I changed Vi back to the interlocking grip, her game quickly improved.

Whatever grip a golfer uses, and this is especially true for the older player, the hands must be in balance. A very strong right hand grip makes a very strong grip with the left hand also necessary. This is why a typical older golfer, whose left hand can't hold onto the club with tremendous force, had better avoid the strong grip. Otherwise, he'll be constantly fighting a hook, because his right hand will constantly be overpowering his left. Such an overpowering of one hand by the other can slightly damage a young player's swing, but it will absolutely destroy that of the older player. He will lose the touch that is such a necessary part of his game. A few teachers have advocated a "hook grip" (where the right hand is way under) for the older player in order to increase power. I consider that a mistake, however. Such an unnatural grip probably won't gain a player any yards, and for the reason I've given, it will very likely cause him to lose accuracy.

The Vardon Grip: This is the grip used by the largest number of players. It consists of an overlapping of the two hands for the purpose of causing them to work comfortably together as a unit. The left hand is placed on the club first, and the club is held securely with the last three fingers of the left hand. This is what is known as the pressure point of the left hand, and it is here that the largest amount of control exists throughout the swing. The right hand is then placed below the left hand and in such a manner that the pocket which is formed between the right thumb and palm fits on top of the left thumb. The little finger of the right hand is overlapped around the middle joint of the forefinger of the left hand. The greatest pressure point for the right hand is between the thumb and index finger, and these become the "feelers" that allow one to determine distance and general touch.

Again, there is individual variation, but normally the left hand grip comes closer to being a palm type of grip, and the right hand grip is closer to being a finger type of grip. This means that the club lies across the roots of the fingers of the left hand and comes to rest near the little finger on what has often been referred to as the "butt-pad." This is a muscular pad which is located at the back of the left hand. As a result when the hand is closed, the club is locked between the roots of the fingers and the palm, and it would surely be correct to state that the club is gripped by the palm and the roots of the fingers. This, of course, means that the grip with the left hand is very securely locked into the palm by the curling action of the fingers around the grip of the club. In the right hand, the club is placed across the middle joint of the fingers, and it does not at any time come close to the palm of the right hand. Now there are some fine players that do grip the club farther down in the right hand, or in other words closer to the palm. They are exceptions, however, and generally speaking the right-hand strength this type of grip provides makes it a strong grip and therefore conducive to hooking. Such a strong grip may work well for an individual player, but its general tendency works against hitting reasonably straight shots. There is, of course, a great deal of theoretical debate as to how much left hand or right hand to use in gripping the club. Generally speaking, again, the average player will see two or two and a half knuckles on his left hand as he looks down over the hand while he grips the club.

Another way to set the hands in the Vardon grip is to point the closed end of the V made by each hand's index finger and thumb in the direction of the right shoulder. But I believe an even better way than that to set the hands when using this grip is as follows. Place the club head on the ground in front of the left leg so that the grip at the top of the club can be rested approximately in the middle of the left thigh. Then bend slightly and grip the club without any turning or twisting of the left hand. The naturalness of the club's position should produce a natural grip with the left hand. And this in turn should produce a natural placement for the right hand, using the Vardon grip, because the pocket formed by the thumb and palm of the right hand then comfortably overlaps the left thumb. You will find that if you grip with the right hand near the palm, you will have what is called a strong right hand grip; that is, the right hand will be farther under the club and will be conducive to a hook. If you grip closer to the fingers with the right hand, the hand will in turn ride up higher or to the left, and you will have the so-called weak right hand grip which is conducive to a slice. You will need to do some experimentation in order to find the grip that produces the type of shot that you wish and provides the largest amount of comfort throughout the swing. Always keep in mind, however, that the main pressures are applied by the last three fingers of the left hand (all but the forefinger and thumb) and the thumb and index finger of the right hand—and that these two pressures should be maintained equally throughout the swing. If right-hand pressure exceeds left-hand pressure, the tendency will be to hook. If the reverse is true, the tendency will be to cancel out the force of the right hand, causing the shot to be weak and some variety of a left to right fade.

While the Vardon Grip is not used by everyone, it is considered a good grip for the average player because of the efficient way it unifies the hands throughout the swing. There is a Vardon grip variation that I like and would suggest that the reader try. This involves a slight separation of the index finger of the right hand away from the other fingers. It is my feeling that this slight separation allows for a greater control and feel with the very important "feelers" on the right hand. I have found that this type of grip works very well for most of the people I have taught. It seems to work especially well for the older player, increasing his feel of the club and therefore adding to his touch control. This particularly helps around the greens.

The Interlocking Grip: In every respect but one, the interlocking grip is identical to the Vardon Grip. The difference is that the little finger of the right hand is interlocked with—instead of lapped over—the forefinger of the left hand. This means the two hands are actually joined together and should, with this type of grip, therefore, work together very well. This is the grip I myself employ. In my teaching experience I have also found that it works very well for people with short fingers. An older player probably should try the Vardon grip first. If this doesn't give him a good touch, he should experiment with the interlocking grip.

The Baseball Grip: The so-called baseball grip is actually a grip employed wherein all ten fingers are placed on the club. There is no interlocking or overlapping of the hands—they aren't joined at all—and generally speaking this grip results in more of a palm grasp by both hands than is true of the two styles already mentioned. There aren't many excellent players who have used this particular grip, and it has never enjoyed the popularity of the other two grips. The major reason for this is that gripping the club in or close to the palms of both hands, produces very little finger control of the club. This lack of control produces wild shots. The argument in favor of the grip is that it adds power to the swing so that an individual may be able to hit the ball farther than he could with the other two grips. I don't believe that argument, and I do not recommend the baseball grip except for those few players who find that it adds distance, accuracy and comfort to their games. I don't feel that the older player should use it merely to gain distance. It may work for a few tour players who play everyday, but that is a vastly different condition that exists for the average amateur player.

Whichever of the three grips, or variations of them, a player uses, he should strive for smoothness, efficiency and consistent repeatability. He should grip the club the same way on all occasions. If there is variation within the grip technique then the player does not develop uniformity of swing, and he will find that his shots vary from one occasion to the next. Good golf needs consistency more than any other one thing. If a player normally slices the ball, he can, to some extent, compensate as needed for the slice. If, however, he slices one ball, hooks the next, and hits the next straight, he never knows what's going to happen or how to compensate. If I had to choose, I would prefer to be able to hit one type of shot consistently as distinct from being able to hit many types of shots, but none of them consistently. Remember, success on the golf course depends on being able to salvage bad shots as well as hit good shots—and one way of salvaging bad shots is being able to compensate for them in advance.

Practice gripping the club until you find the technique that gives you the best chance of success, and it is quite likely that you will find a self-repeating grip that makes you swing constant and gradually improves your scores. Above all, do not vary your grip from one shot to the next, and always remember that golf is a game that employs both hands. Use one hand to the exclusion of the other, or allow one hand to dominate the other, and you're bound to have constant trouble. You'll never be able to score consistently well until you know what the ball is likely to do when you hit it; and that knowledge starts with a sound grip. As an older player try to develop touch, control and rhythm. Don't go for those few extra yards at the expense of accuracy. Work towards finesse, and never try to overpower the ball.

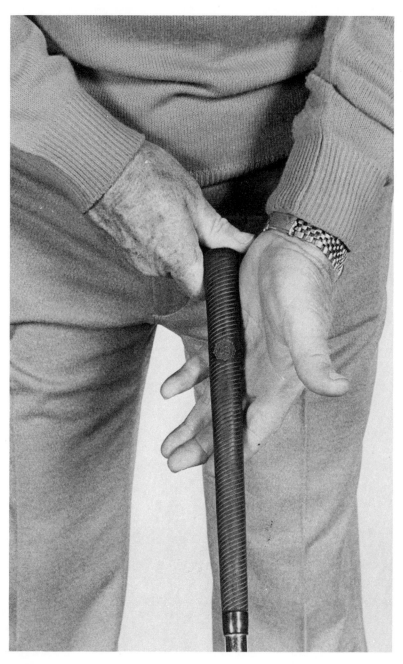

Procedure for placement of the left hand in the Vardon grip.

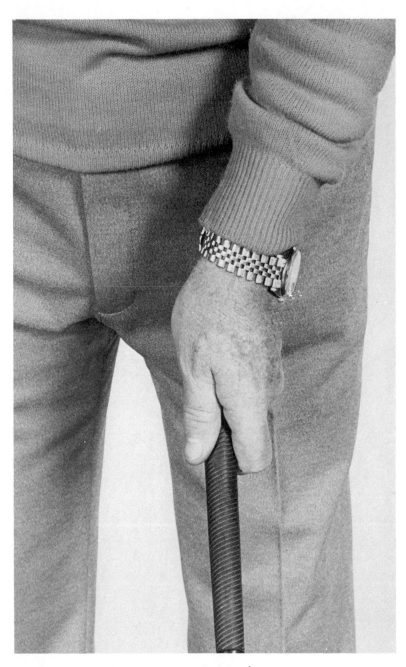

Placement of the left hand in the Vardon grip.

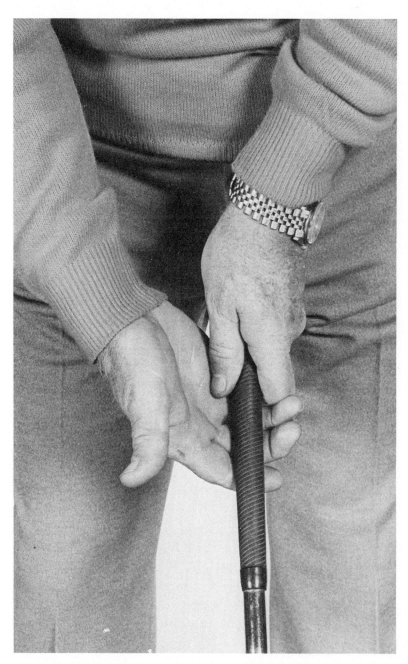

Procedure for placement of the right hand in the Vardon grip.

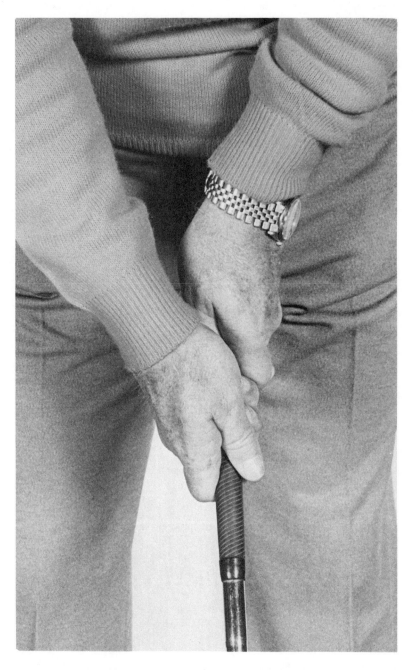

Placement of both hands in the Vardon grip — front view.

Back view of the hands in the Vardon grip.

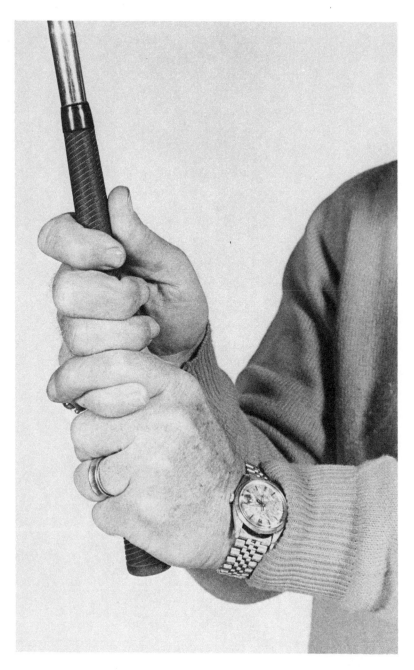

Placement of hands in the interlocking grip.

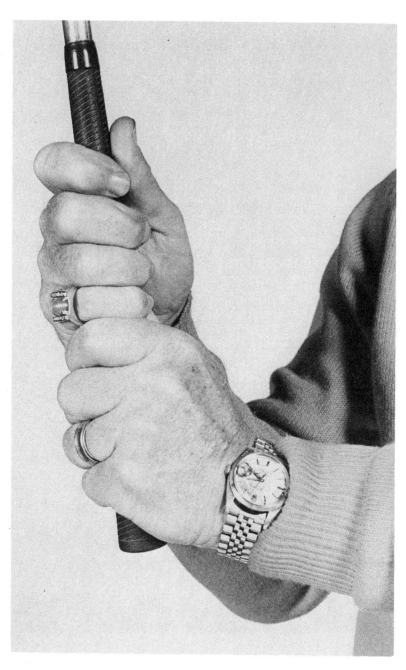

The baseball grip.

The "V's" formed by the thumb and index finger of both hands should point near the right shoulder.

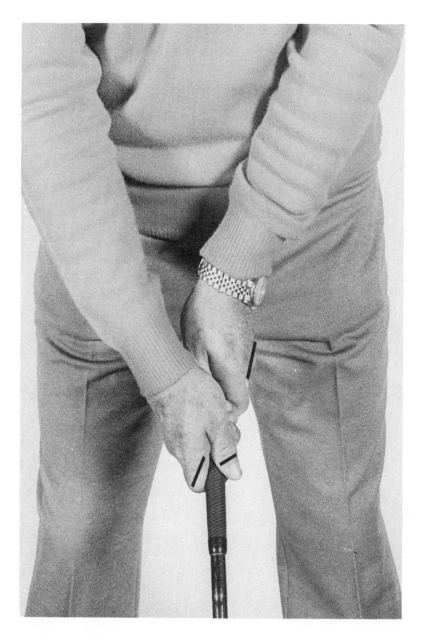

"Pressure points" of the grip. The club is held securely with the last three fingers of the left hand, and the thumb and index finger of the right hand.

4

The Set-Up:
What Happens with Age?

*Develop a natural set-up, by adopt-
ing a comfortable posture, taking a
firm stance and bending to release
shoulder tension.*

There are three phases of a golf swing: the address, the backswing and the
downswing. In this chapter we will focus on the first, the set-ups, and will
show how it affects the other two parts. We will also talk about changes
that take place in the set-up with advancing age.

To begin with a few remarks about the set-up in general, regardless
of age, most golf books and magazine articles that deal with the swing
devote numerous pages to the backswing, still more to the downswing
and only a few to the address. Writers become very involved in countless
theories about backswing planes, downswing planes, shoulder action and
follow through. Yet nearly all of these patterns are established as soon
as the player sets himself up in front of the ball. Watch a touring
professional next time there is a televised golf presentation and note the
amount of time that he takes getting set up. He fully realizes that he
can never hit consistently good shots without a proper set-up. More than
that, he knows that what follows in the swing is dictated by his set-up.
In my years of teaching I have found that about 90 percent of missed
shots occur because of some fault going right back to the address position.

The question then becomes one of the changes that need to be
made in the general set-up as a result of age. Time and time again
throughout this book the reader will note that we hark back to psychology. I do this for two reasons: because golf is mainly a mental game,

and because I believe that mainly the older player is harmed by negative thinking. He believes he is handicapped, and he therefore *creates* a handicap. Youth on the other hand carries with it a certain cockiness. The young player tends to become careless because he thinks he can do anything. He doesn't recognize his human shortcomings, and while this has some liability it also has its advantages. Confidence is a great asset to the golfer.

Older persons do frequently have some difficulty with their concentration. This may perhaps be a part of the aging process, but I believe that it is primarily related to numerous business interests. There is also a great tendency in our society to dwell upon ill health, however, and this too becomes a distraction.

The first thing this means for an older golfer is that he should not take an excessively long period of time in setting up over the ball. He should plan his shot, select his club, and then get right to his set-up. He should work to get to the point where he quickly and easily sets-up—in exactly the same way for every shot. He may have to devote more concentration in the beginning to establish the right pattern for him. He may, for example, practice his set-up procedure a few minutes in his home in the evenings. He will definitely need to work harder on the mental aspect of his set-up. If he allows negative thoughts to creep into his mind he will very likely tense up and in some manner change his set-up pattern or procedure. This is why we believe he should not take an undue period of time to set-up over the ball. Too much time allows for too much thinking, whereas a good set-up should be natural and automatic. As the set-up becomes more automatic it will also become more consistent and self-repeating.

I am reminded of one of my older students who was constantly concerned about distance. He seemed to believe that he had lost many yards as he had aged. I did not see evidence of that on the practice tee. One day, however, I joined him on the course just at the time when he was fretting about a long approach shot to the green. I could figuratively see the wheels going around in his head as he worried about his club selection. Tension set in, and by the time he finally hit the shot he was too tense to make a smooth movement through the ball. It was obvious to me that he had lost yardage, not because of age but because of worry. His set-up was slow because of his enormous indecision, and the very slowness of the process gave him far too much time to worry.

I am not advocating quickness at the expense of thoroughness. I have already stated that I believe the set-up to be the most vital part of the swing—and perhaps even the entire game. It is even more crucial for the older person because he must attain maximum result from minimum effort. The younger person can sometimes make up for error by utilizing brute force. If he hits the ground behind the ball, for example, he may have sufficient strength to force the club through the ball—and compensate for the fat shot. The older man probably won't have that kind of strength. Perhaps, too, the older man must use everything he has in order to drive the ball 250 yards. The younger man may be able to get that with a weak hit.

There is another point to be stressed too. Perhaps with age an individual finds that he can no longer bend over the ball with as much agility as he could when he was younger. This dictates a postural change for the older player. He needs to recognize this so that he can find *his* normal, comfortable position. It may be very different from what it was when he was younger. That's fine according to my principle of building the game around the individual, not the individual around the game.

All of this adds up to a special need for mental discipline by the older player. He should find the set-up that works well and feels comfortable. Then he should find some way of duplicating it each time he sets-up to the ball. And he should adopt a pace in setting up that is unhurried enough to allow for care but quick enough to facilitate mental and physical relaxation.

So much for variations with age. What then, is *the* proper set-up?

I am thoroughly convinced that there isn't one right set-up if we are talking about arm position, or leg position of any one stance. Most golf writers teach a set-up such as the one they use and they claim that this is *the* correct one for everyone to use. That, I feel, is a very absurd position to take. What if I were six feet eight inches tall? Would the average man, of say five feet eight, be expected to stand as I do? Of course not. I am close to average height and weight, but I still do not teach a set-up such as the one I use. Mine works for me, but it will not work well for most other players because of individual differences. When I decided to write this book, I also decided to use my normal teaching methods and to approach the game in a highly individualized manner. The concept that there is only one mold in which everyone must be modeled is foreign to my methods. This makes the writing more difficult because I can't simply stress one method as being correct for everyone. My job becomes one of helping each individual find those ingredients that are correct for him because they will enable him to maximize his natural ability.

Golf is essentially a natural game. The goal in hitting longer shots is to be able to swing a club with maximum force and minimum effort. An older player who tries to force a shot with maximum effort operates at a distinct disadvantage. He creates tension and destroys his swing. The club hits the ball; the player doesn't do it. A player who mistakenly thinks he is the main ingredient in striking a golf ball will lunge at the ball and try to force the shot. He'll lose rhythm and his shot will fail. In order to swing the club properly a player *must* be relaxed. Otherwise, his muscles are tied up, his backswing becomes jerky and his downswing will not produce maximum club head speed. He will try to resort to strength, and this will add to his disadvantage.

How can anyone be relaxed if he is forced to stand or move in an unnatural way? Any 10 different sets of hands have physical differences. The same is true for shoulder construction, leg and hip size, and general body build and carriage. I estimate, from years of observation, that only one person in a 100 walks with a completely straight left arm at his side. Most people let their arms hang loosely, with a slightly bent elbow, when they relax and walk. Yet most golfers are taught to have a left arm that is as straight as a yard stick. I say this is unnatural and breeds tension, discomfort, and finally, discouragement. My principle of molding the golf game around the individual and not the reverse applies even more to the set-up than to most other aspects of the game. I will frequently suggest that a player stand naturally and note the position of his arms, shoulders and so forth. This demonstrates his natural position, the one he should maintain throughout his set-up. The two positions should be very similar and will go far toward providing the naturalness for which we strive. Above all then a golf student must constantly ask himself, "Do I feel comfortable and relaxed?" We need to add that we are interested in his posture *now* and we aren't concerned with what he looked like as a younger man.

The first part of the set-up involves placing the hands on the club. Obviously a player can't begin a set-up until he's taken a hold on the club. I talked about the variations in the grip in the previous chapter. The point here is to place the club, once it's properly grasped, in a position relative to the ball and the body. I suggest as a first move placement of the left hand on the club. This is done by placing the club behind the ball, bending slightly to reduce shoulder strain and securing the grip that a player has selected as most comfortable. Start with the feet close together and then bend over from the waist to the point where there is no strain across the chest. The angle between the target and the direction in which the feet point should be 90°, establishing the front of the body perpendicular to the target line. Once a player bends over the ball he should have established his arm position, and here again the major goal is comfort and relaxation.

There are two main questions that I find often asked of me: at this point in the set-up position, how much to bend over and how far to stand from the ball? Taking them in reverse order, I do not believe that there is any one formula for determining how far to stand from the ball. I have often heard the rule that the end of the club, or butt of the grip should be a distance of one open hand from the thigh. I do not believe this is even a good general rule because of the variation of people's physiques. If we like general rules we might say that a woman should reach more than a man because during the swing her arms must not be restricted by her bust. The rule that I use is to stand so that the arms hang naturally from the body. Most players tend to reach too much, and by so doing they pull the arms out and away from the body.

As to the question of how much to bend over the ball, the rule is again one of naturalness. If a person's arms normally hang in a very straight manner when he walks, he should bend until they assume that same position. But such a person is the exception. Most people have a slight bend at the elbows, when their arms hang naturally, and that should therefore be their position as they address the ball. Any unusual tightness will create tension that will lock the muscles and thereby prevent a smooth, unrestricted, rhythmical backswing. There is an interesting and useful checkpoint that can be used. Once the arms are positioned you should be able to stand up again and hold the club out straight in front of your body. You will immediately see if that would be your normal way of holding some object. The only unnatural thing about a golf stance is the golf club that's being held while bending over. The reason a golfer bends at the waist, in fact, is to release any tightness through the chest that comes from holding the club.

The next point in the set-up is placing the feet in position. This will of course vary with the club being used. A driver requires playing the ball approximately off the left heel. Stance will be shoulder width, which means that the distance from the inside of the feet should equal the outside width of the shoulders. We need to maintain balance all through a drive, and for that reason the stance must be sufficiently wide so that a player will not lurch toward his right side on the backswing or his left side on the downswing. Too wide a stance, on the other hand, makes it difficult to move the weight back to the right on the backswing.

After securing the proper width for his stance, the player needs to pay some attention to the placement of his feet and legs. I strongly suggest an even weight distribution between the two feet. This maintains balance and also facilitates a smooth backswing. After all, a player must shift weight from one foot to the other in order to generate power. If the weight is already heavily upon the right foot, there is no more weight to shift there. Too much weight on the left foot, at the address, makes it impossible to shift most of the weight over to the right side on the backswing.

I suggest the following simple procedures to the reader. Make an effort to get your weight evenly distributed on both feet. Plant your feet firmly just as if you were standing in mud. Do not put your weight back on your heels, for you will then destroy your balance and lose the ability to transfer your weight. Keep the weight distributed over the whole length of each foot, giving you the feeling that you are well anchored to the ground. This is vital for the older person since his body movement is usually slowed with age.

There are a number of variations too as far as the position of the feet. I prefer to have the left foot open, about half way between pointing at the target and pointing at a right angle from the target. This enables me to move easily through the ball. If the left foot is square to the ball, a player runs the risk of placing strain upon his ankle as he moves through his swing. The case of the right foot is altogether different, since a player only moves weight *to* the right foot on the backswing. Weight should never move to the outside of the right foot, nor should the hips rotate beyond the point in the backswing where their circular motion can be smoothly stopped and reversed. If the hips go beyond that point, or if the weight shifts too far to the right, a player won't be able to quickly and smoothly reverse the direction of his movement and get into a good downswing. This is especially vital for the older player.

For these reasons I like the square right foot, which establishes the front of the body perpendicular to the target line. These are only suggestions, however, and any restriction they cause in the swing is a good reason for modifying or abandoning them. The ideal swing, again, is a free-flowing, unrestricted transfer of weight, first moving to the right and then moving back in the same arc to the left.

Correct knee posture is another vital ingredient of a good swing. The legs provide a basic foundation for the body as it shifts back and forth, so the legs have to move. And it's impossible to get good leg action with stiff or locked knees. There must be some flex in the knees at all times. A player gets this flex by bending his knees at the address position just as he would if he were carrying a fairly heavy object. In addition the right knee should be pointed in toward the center of the stance or in the direction of the ball. This is done for several reasons. It prevents the weight from going to the outside of the right foot at the top of the backswing. It also deters the hips from turning too far around on the backswing.

The address cannot be completed until the player has selected the type of stance that he wishes to use. This should not be too difficult a choice since there are only three varieties. A square stance is one in which both feet are equidistant from the ball, with both toes touching that perpendicular line to the target I've already mentioned. If we are talking pure theory we could say that this stance results in a straight ball. That is not a realistic statement, however, since very few people will *ever* hit an absolutely straight ball. It is unquestionably the most difficult shot in golf and requires near perfect timing. The best statement would be that the square stance in and of itself will not produce either a hook or a slice. I have no criticism of that statement, and would only add that if the square stance feels comfortable for you, use it in good faith.

The closed stance is one in which the left foot is placed ahead of the right foot, or closer to the ball than the right foot. Such a position will encourage a greater turning action of the body than the square stance, and particularly a turning of the hips on the backswing. The club will go more sharply inside the target line on the backswing. On the downswing it will also be more difficult to move rapidly through the ball, however. The closed stance will therefore encourage an inside-out swing. This is conducive to a hook, although again there are many other factors that will dictate whether or not a player hooks the ball. Many fine players use the closed stance with distance clubs, the driver and fairway woods. Generally, it is not used with the irons since the tendency then would be to get too much hook. When driving from a closed stance, the golfer's left foot should be no more than two inches ahead of his right foot. A left foot farther ahead than that will normally produce a *big* hook. I would suggest this stance to a player who has difficulty getting the weight back to his right foot. Along with comfort, the controlling factor in selecting this stance is whether a hooking type of shot is desired. If a person tends to hook too much already, or if his hips tend to turn too far around on the backswing, then the closed stance isn't for him.

The third variety of stance is the open stance. Here, the right foot is placed ahead of the left foot. Driving from this stance, like driving from the closed stance, has limits for positioning the feet—the right foot should be no more than two inches closer to the ball than the left foot. As I will note in a later chapter, this is the stance generally used for most of the irons. The rule of thumb is that the open stance is conducive to a left-to-right shot. I do not like to say *slice* because a sliding type shot can produce excellent results. The ball just gradually slides to the right and it will still get plenty of roll when it hits the ground.

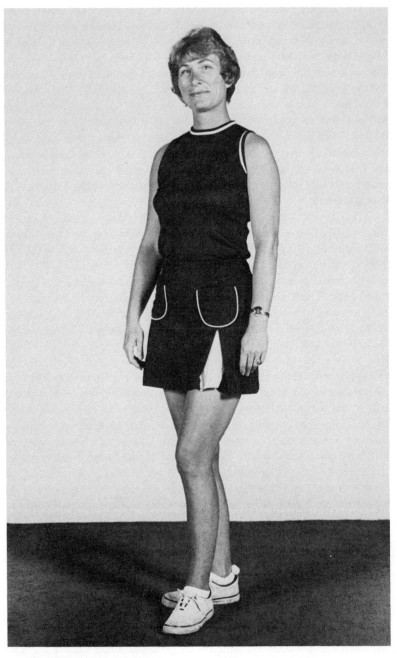

Relaxed posture setup.

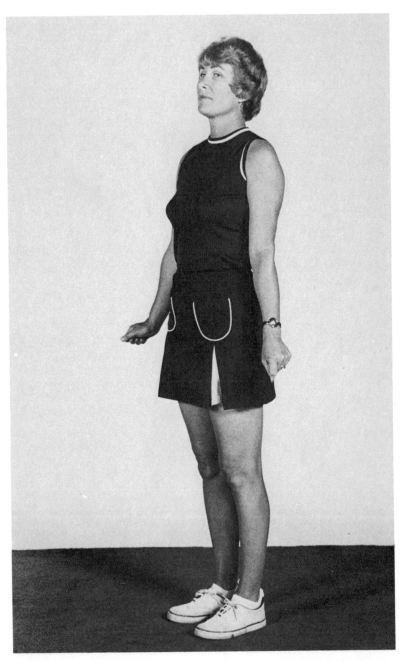

Tense posture setup.

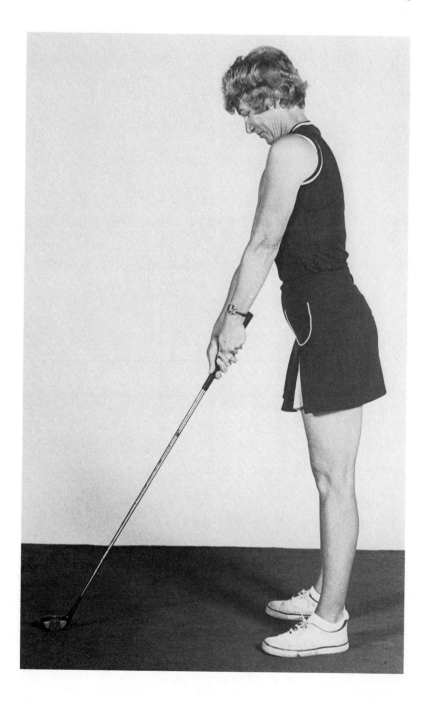

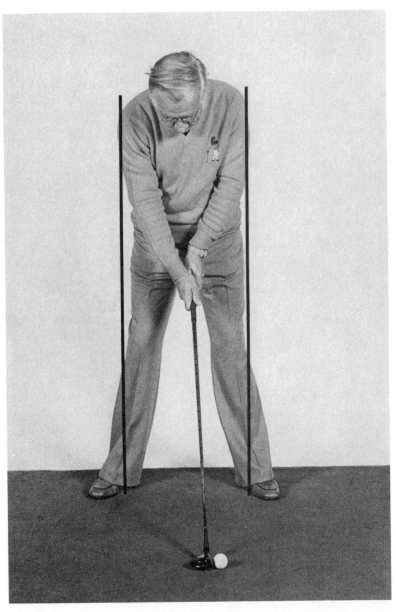

The placement of the feet forms a foundation for the swing. A wide stance helps provide balance and the correct width for each player is determined by the width of his shoulders. The distance from the inside of the feet should be equal to the outside width of the shoulders.

Feet should be placed solidly on the ground with the weight carried along the whole foot. The golfer's arms should hang naturally from the shoulders, and knees should be slightly bent. You can never make a consistently good move back from the ball nor down and through the ball if you lock your knees at any time during the swing.

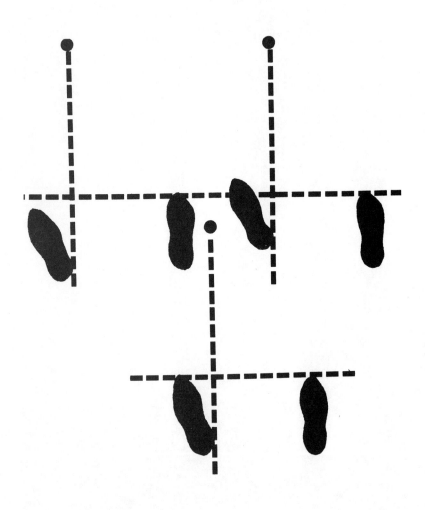

Ball placement is closely linked to body position. Your body should line up with your stance. Whether the player uses the open, closed or square stance depends on the individual's choice.

Elbow position for the set-up. Although experts disagree as to whether the elbows should point down toward the hips or outward, I feel that a player should position his elbows as he normally does, bending enough so that the shoulders are relaxed.

Many fine players achieve excellent results with this shot, even though the slice is generally considered a weak shot. The open stance will cause a somewhat more upright swing and will not encourage the hips to roll way around on the backswing. A major advantage to the open stance, at the same time, is that it allows the player to move quickly through the ball on the downswing. This is of great importance since weight transfer through the ball provides not only more distance but also greater accuracy. Since this is a great asset to the older player it should be considered. The open stance, therefore, comes highly recommended; a player should definitely try it, and establish it as his normal stance if it produces the kind of shot and feel that a player likes.

Ball placement with respect to the feet is still another vital consideration in the set-up. Ball position varies according to the club selected and the type of shot that is planned. More will be mentioned about ball placement in a subsequent chapter. Here, I wish to merely indicate the importance of ball placement. Suppose, for example, that a golfer preparing to drive, places the ball outside the left foot. This will cause the player to reach for the ball at the time of impact, and therefore will pose an especially severe problem for the older player since his body generally moves slower and with less agility than it did when he was younger. It is very likely that the player will find himself lunging at the ball. His head will move forward and he may top the ball, pop it into the air or hit it either right or left. He will not be likely to get good distance, and he'll hit many bad shots.

On the other hand, suppose he plays his driver from the middle of his stance. He will now have to pick the club up on the backswing since the shoulders and arms cannot be timed in sequence with the hips. Coming back down into the ball he will feel crowded and all cramped up. He can't hit against a strong left side and generally he will chop down on the ball. From this position he will likely hit a variety of bad shots, but seldom a good one.

These seemingly minor changes in ball placement will greatly influence the type of shot hit. Reaching for the ball, for example, will put the player on his toes at impact and therefore make him very much off balance. Standing too close, on the other hand, will produce a high, weak shot to the right. Careless ball placement, in short, will make a golfer's shots notably inconsistent.

The final part of the set-up involves alignment of the ball toward a target. By the time a player has positioned body, club and ball, it only remains for him to place his feet so that they are square to the target line. A square stance, again, makes both feet perpendicular to the target line. An open stance keeps only the right foot perpendicular to that line, while a closed stance keeps only the left foot perpendicular to it. In no case would a golfer's feet ever be placed so that they aim directly toward the target. Since the body and the ball are not on the same line, a player must also keep his feet parallel with the direction his body is facing—and aim slightly to the left of his target.

To review a few of the points that have been presented here, one important set-up factor is the pace—good set-up takes adequate time, but once the swing begins it takes only about one-half second to hit the ball. I don't care how quick a mind any person has; nobody can both act and think in half a second. The swing must flow automatically, therefore, and without thought.

My main advice to the reader is this: be natural. The only way you can do this is by adapting your set-up to your physique. Forget the straight left arm and also the straight line from the left shoulder to the club head, unless that is your natural position. Pay very close attention to your normal walking posture. Line yourself up according to that, not according to pictures that you have seen of some of the players on the professional tour. The players in the pictures may not be built anything like you are, and generally they won't be your age. The only unnatural thing about setting-up to hit a golf ball is that you are bending over. Bend enough to release any tension in the shoulders and arms. Take a firm stance with your feet and keep your knees flexed so that your movement is free and easy. Keep the right knee bent in, so that the weight will not flow to the outside of the right foot at the top of the backswing. Be relaxed and confident. If you have done what I have suggested, you have every reason to be sure you will do well. You must practice your set-up so that it repeats itself with consistency. By standardizing your address position you will find that you have developed swing continuity, a vital factor to good golf. A very minor error in your set-up will become magnified in the backswing and in the downswing, increasing the effect of the original error. Errors must be corrected at the beginning and if you do that you will have eliminated by far the greatest source of badly hit shots!

5

The Backswing

Keep the backswing simple, with shorter moves, one-piece action and consistent rhythm.

The second part of the golf swing is the backswing. The purpose of the backward swinging action is to move the club to a position behind the golfer from which he can generate a solid forward swing through the ball with maximum power. I want to emphasize the word *swing* because it is important to realize that a golfer does not directly hit the ball; he swings a club. It's the club that hits the ball. The swing needs to be smooth and there should never be a time during the downswing when a player tries to force his hands into a shot. Good rhythm during the downswing actually starts during the backswing. A jerky backswing will destroy the rhythm of the downswing. The game of golf consists of a chain of small consecutive movements that work together and blend into large movements—so a bad move anywhere at the beginning of the chain affects the end of the chain too.

There are some very important changes that take place with the backswing as a person becomes older. I have talked all along about naturalness, and nowhere is this more needed than in the backswing. One of the most important bodily changes that takes place with age involves flexibility. As we grow older, the joints have a tendency to stiffen and we do not move as easily as we once did.

That means any movement that was unnatural when we were young will be even more unnatural and difficult as we become older. A young person, for example, who sways the weight to the outside of the right foot on the backswing will have trouble moving his weight through the ball on the downswing. He may still get enough of his weight through the ball, despite the difficulty, to play fairly consistent golf. With age he will find consistent golf virtually impossible. The point is that natural-ness becomes crucial for the older player. The swing must of necessity become more compact as the player grows older.

There is one area, however, where age can work to our advantage if we will only allow it to do so. The loss of some of the flexibility in joints automatically shortens the backswing. I have seen a few older players actually trying to lengthen their backswing so that they could hit with as much power as they did when they were younger.

Several years ago, for example, a 58-year-old man came to me in mental agony; he couldn't hit the ball any distance at all. I watched his practice swing and immediately found the trouble. He was keeping his club head parallel to the ground for too long a time as he brought it back, and in so doing was swaying off the ball. He thought he could regain yardage by lengthening the backswing, but he actually lost dis-tance. He began to hit far more distance when I succeeded in getting him to use the more compact backswing dictated by age.

This compactness is natural for an older player. It might not have been so when the player was younger, but what is natural at one age may well *not* be natural and comfortable at another age.

I recommend that an older player accept the shorter backswing not only as natural, in fact, but also as beneficial to his game. I question whether backswing shortness *per se* cuts down stroke distance, anyway, at least to any appreciable extent. Backswing shortness actually makes the whole swing more compact, and a compact swing is a much more consistent swing if we are playing fewer rounds of golf and practicing less. The player with a short backswing should also find that he is hitting a higher percentage of good shots, which is what golf finally comes down to. So in the case of the backswing, the changes an older player is forced to make should actually improve his game—meaning that age is then working for us rather than against us.

The backswing in general, apart from the effects age has on it, can be destroyed by too much thinking. The old adage that "analysis breeds paralysis" applies well to the backswing. A golf swing must be one continuous motion with all parts moving in synchronization. A negative thought will create tension which in turn tightens muscles and blocks the free flow of the motion. For example, watch what happens if the right side tightens prior to the backswing. You will find it very difficult to move the club back at all. In fact you will find it difficult and uncomfortable even to *begin* the backswing. For that reason, I do not believe that a player should delay his backswing for any appreciable period of time once he has completed his set-up. There aren't many successful players who stand over the ball for a long time. The majority do not delay because they want to get the show on the road before the tension begins to build up—which it surely will do if you stand there and think. There is simply no place in a backswing for thinking; you must learn to relax, have faith in your set-up and trust to your muscle memory to do the rest.

Nearly all fine players begin their backswing with some sort of waggle or extraneous movement. The purpose of this is to keep the muscles slightly in motion so they don't tighten up. The waggle involves an abbreviated swinging of the club with the hands and arms prior to the start of the backswing. I don't care what sort of waggle a golfer uses so long as he uses something of the sort. Most players naturally find their own waggle. I suggest a back and forth movement of the club so that the weight of the club head is felt, and to keep the wrists and other parts of the upper body slightly in motion. And even though the club will again be at rest immediately prior to the backswing I still consider that waggle to be part of the backswing. Anything that has to go into a backswing logically becomes an integral part of that backswing.

I have seen many players ruin a whole swing right after the waggle. Doubt creeps into their minds, causing backswing to be delayed. It is as if they had developed a plan of action, selected a club, set themselves up over the ball, waggled, and then—after all that—had tried to second-guess themselves. This is an absolutely disastrous error almost always ruining the shot that follows. What happens is that after a golfer spends all that time planning, a split second later he rejects the whole plan. How can anyone be likely to come up with a sound alternate plan in only a split second?

Second guessing, besides being incapable of producing any well planned action itself, actually forces errors to happen. The pattern golfers generally develop prior to starting their backswings, as I mentioned earlier, varies—but as an example let's say it involves three waggles and no pause. Now if the three-waggle golfer pauses after the third one, he has changed his whole pattern. Tension then creeps into his body and his backswing will probably be jerky. What a golfer should do if a pause creeps in and changes his established waggling procedure is to back away from the ball and start the whole procedure all over again. Better yet, he should train himself always to suppress negative thoughts and doubts. A golfer must develop confidence in himself and go with what he has.

A

The first moves of the backswing, showing a one-piece swing.

B

He must *never* delay his backswing once he has completed his waggle.

Several questions I keep hearing are: "What do I move first in my backswing? Do I start with my hips? Do my arms move first? Or is it the shoulders that begin the move backwards?" Some theorists have talked about a chain of movements starting with the hands and arms; then involving the shoulders, hips, and legs. It is my contention that the human mind cannot think of all of these movements and still synchronize them into a unit. For example, none of the analysts specify how *far* the hands move before the shoulders move nor how any two other movements are phsycially and chronologically related.

I said earlier that I want to make the golf swing as simple as possible. Consistent to this central idea is my concept that the backswing starts with everything moving *together* as a unit. The backswing *must* be a one-piece affair or else the whole swing will be ruined. I recognize that individuals have different beliefs about what initiates the backswing. My point is that whether the process starts with one action or another doesn't really make any difference. What really matters is that every action and every part of the body moves together synchronously. I refer to this as the "one-unit backswing" and it is from this that virtually all the timing of the swing is established.

There is another very controversial point about the backswing: the speed, or tempo, at which the club is moved back. In most golf books you will find a rule stating that the backswing must be very slow and smooth. I agree with the *smooth* part of that rule.

I most certainly do not agree with the *slow* part. By way of illustrating the weakness I find in an excessively slow backswing, I once had a student come to me with the problem that he was jumping at the ball on his downswing. He found himself moving his head forward and as a result lunging at the ball. He felt perplexed because he knew that he had a good-looking swing, he knew what his fault was, but he didn't know why. I immediately noticed that he had an extremely slow and deliberate backswing and I asked him about that. He had been told that his backswing was too fast and he had therefore set about correcting this "grievous error." I noticed this man walking to the practice tee at a very rapid pace. All of his movements were rapid, in fact, from gripping the club to setting up to the ball. This told me that his normal pace in life was rapid. His natural golf swing also was fast, and his great desire to put everything into his shots caused him to speed up his downswing. It was as if he were driving a car 10 miles an hour on his backswing and then shooting it up to 100 miles an hour on the downswing. There simply had to be a jerk somewhere in the man's swing.

I explained to him that the purpose of the backswing is to get the club far enough back so that it can deliver an effective downswing. He began to hit excellent shots as soon as the tempo of his backswing increased.

I do feel that a backswing can be too fast, but only in two circumstances. One is when a golfer's backswing is so fast that it forces him off balance on the backswing. The other is when a backswing is so fast that it destroys the one-unit swing. I tell my students to think of a backswing as a door: you can open the door quickly or slowly; but, either way, all parts of that door move together. As long as you don't rip the door off its hinges, you won't be opening or closing it too fast.

As mentioned in an earlier chapter, too tight a grip will produce tension that will in turn restrict the free flow a backswing needs. Too loose a grip, on the other hand, makes it possible to lose the club on the backswing. What I want to reemphasize here is that your grip pressure should never be varied once the backswing begins. It should remain uniform all through the swing.

The backswing itself is a simple move that transfers the weight from the left side to the right side. The weight is about evenly divided between the two legs at address; at the top of the backswing about 80 percent of the weight will be on the right leg. I do not like to say the backswing is a *turn* because that implies it is like a baseball swing. In actuality there is a large turn of the shoulders and about half as much (or even less for many players) turn of the hips. The first movements carry the weight directly over to the right leg and this is most certainly not a turning motion. If a player insists on turning those hips far around to the right, he'll be so far out of position that the hips can't slide on the downswing. As an older player this big hip turn will be most unnatural because such a turn demands great flexibility.

The theory isn't as important as what actually happens during the backswing, however. A golfer who keeps his head in its original position, goes back in one piece and keeps his knees flexed will find that his shoulders are turning greatly while his hips aren't turning much at all. And all this happens automatically, from the set-up and the one-piece backswing. The bend in the knees prevents the hips from making a big turn to the right. The right knee, braced in toward the ball at the very beginning prevents the weight from going to the outside of the right foot. It also restricts the movement of the hips. These set-up moves will automatically have produced tension on the inside of the right leg which in turn will wind up like a spring at the top of the backswing position. From this a golfer will be able to generate leg power at the vary start of his downswing. He will allow the hips to move around on the backswing only to the point where the left knee points at the ball. Going beyond that point always prevents a player from moving back through the ball—at the proper time—in his downswing. And this bad timing, in turn, causes the player to hit off his right foot and therefore without any power.

The position of the head during the backswing is important. We all have heard remarks about a shot being ruined because the player "took his eye off the ball." I believe this is nonsense, or at best a misunderstanding of what is important in regard to head position. After all, I can easily keep my eye on the ball (which merely means to watch the ball) and still move my head far to the right. In that case my head has come "off the ball" according to golf terminology, which means the body has been swayed to the right. I feel it is very important to keep the head on the ball during the backswing because if you sway going back you are likely to sway coming down into the ball.

Some older golfers find that they must move their heads to the right side on the backswing. These individuals are not highly flexible through the shoulders. They don't bend, twist, or turn as readily as does the younger person. They have found a sway is necessary for them to be able to make any movement back on the backswing. Swaying, then, is natural for them: I don't advocate this move, but if it is necessary I go along with it. A number of very fine players have used this kind of movement, thereby illustrating that there is almost no inviolate rule in golf. A swayer will simply have to work doubly hard to avoid moving off the ball on the downswing.

Golfers generally are well read people and it is likely they have often come across the word "extension." I have frequently been asked, "How can I get greater extension so I can get more distance?" The question is logical because both distance and accuracy depend to a certain extent on extension on the backswing. But like so many truths, this one can be overemphasized. Extension merely means that the club extends far away from the hands on the backswing. "How can a player lose extension?" would be a more appropriate question than asking how to increase extension.

One way of losing extension is the failure to transfer weight to the right foot at the beginning of the backswing. This action shortens the arc, causing the club to pop up in the air rather than traveling reasonably low and near the ground. But the major culprit is the breaking loose of some joint, principally the wrists. In other words, the club is picked up and not swung back in one piece. There should be no cocking of the wrists below waist level. There won't be if you make the one-unit backswing.

A

The sequence of the moves on the backswing. In photo A, the one piece backswing with the upper part of the body moving ahead of the hips. Photo B shows the movement back as the club nears shoulder height. Photo C illustrates a gradual building up of power by coiling the right leg. In photo D, the backswing is completed. Weight is shown by the dotted line and is carried on the inside of the right leg and foot. This produces a coil type of action so that the player can spring off the right leg on the downswing.

B

C

D

Once again, though, we go back to the importance of the set-up. One player I knew had a tightness across his shoulders. The cramped condition did not allow his joints to remain fixed and somewhere a joint always gave way and bent. As a result, the club was picked up sharply into the air and extension was sharply reduced. So here again, what may sound quite complicated really isn't so involved. In fact, it is automatic if there is a good set-up and a one-piece move on the backswing. Start in one piece for only 12 little inches and you are likely to have success. That first 12 inches are the key to the whole backswing, provided the set-up is good.

The remainder of the backswing simply amounts to a let-it-happen approach. We have accomplished what we set out to do by making the address natural and the start of the backswing correct. There is neither time nor need for any further thinking. One move follows another. Even as I talk about the automatic quality of the backswing, however, I realize that some people are interested in the arc of the backswing. They want to know whether they should swing flat or upright and which of the two is the better position.

Loosely speaking, an upright swing is one in which the club is well above the right shoulder at the top of the backswing. It may be above the middle of the neck, but it should generally not be directly above the head. Usually we look at the position of the hands at the top of the backswing in order to fix the club position more easily. With a flat position the hands will be near the right shoulder, but again, generally should not be below the right shoulder. Again, this is only a *general* rule because a person of unusual build (one in a 100) might deviate slightly from this procedure.

As a rule, tall people use a more upright swing and shorter players use a flatter swing. This is because the shorter man with shorter arms carries the club more with the body and, thus, it goes further around to his right. The reverse, of course, is true for the taller player. A golfer must therefore be guided by his individual physique and swing pattern. Thus the correct arc is the one that naturally follows a correct set-up and one-piece backswing given your particular build.

However, if you reach too far for the ball, farther than is natural for your build, you will flatten your arc too much; and if you stand closer to the ball than is natural for one of your build, you will swing in too upright a way. In either case you will have made an error at the address position. The way to deal with this is not to worry about the end result but to correct the fault at the beginning.

The other major error that can change a player's arc is independent hand or arm movement. Such movement violates, of course, the one-piece backswing, and can be traced back to such errors at the address position as locked shoulder blades. Whatever the cause, if the independent hand or arm movement began in the set-up then it must also be corrected there. If it was solely caused by a two-piece backswing, then it must be dealt with there. My point is that no one *ever* needs to worry about his backswing arc if he sets up properly and begins the backswing correctly.

The same sort of thing is true about the position of the left wrist at the top of the backswing. The position of that wrist dictates whether the club face is open, closed or square at the top of the backswing. A fine player may use any one of the three positions, but what is more important than which position he uses is how he gets there. If he gets to one of the wrist positions because he is out of position at the address, the probable net result of his backswing will be a poor shot. There are many possible causes for bad wrist position at the top, but reaching for the ball and standing too close to it are two common ones.

My advice to anyone who wishes to avoid bad wrist position at the top of the swing is first to set up properly and second to eliminate all independent wrist movement on the backswing. Do these two things and it doesn't matter which of the three wrist positions you determine as best for yourself. On the other hand, if you try to imitate someone else you will lose your own naturalness. You are likely to find that unless you play nearly every day your game will fall apart. That is the price you pay for forcing yourself into a mold.

Let us briefly summarize what should take place by the time the backswing has been completed. We want a smooth, even tempo, a one-piece swing that will carry the club to the right side. We want that weight transferred predominately to the inside of the right leg. The left heel will come off the ground, but no more than two inches. If the heel comes up too high there is generally a loss of balance and it becomes more difficult to transfer immediately the weight back to the left foot at the start of the downswing. The right knee should not be locked: Maintain the flexed position so you can quickly shift the weight back on the downswing. In fact, all the moves of the backswing are designed to be able to shove off from that right leg and move solidly into the ball.

We also want to try to get a full shoulder turn with minimal movement of the hips. Above all, though, a player must complete the backswing before he starts his downswing. If he does not, he won't have the weight to transfer, his timing will be badly off, and he'll very likely jump at the ball. I have seen many players miss shots because they have been so anxious about the shot that they rushed everything. Developing patience and concentrating more than ever on rhythm can pay very great rewards to the older golfer.

I have already stated that I believe we can make the normal aging process work for us in at least one very important way. The automatic reduction of backswing length should help consistency. There may be individuals who can't comfortably shorten the length of their backswings. These people are unusually flexible and do not seem to lose this flexibility very much as a result of age. Consistent with my individual approach to the game of golf, however, I do not insist that everyone shorten his backswing. There are some really fine players who use a very long backswing and often their timing is ruined if they shorten up. I have only two thoughts about the long backswing. First, it will take more practice in order to keep it grooved. Second, if it is long because of some error in the swing, then I am opposed to it. Chief among these errors would be looseness. Be sure to keep a firm grip on the club, especially with the last three fingers of the left hand. If you become loose at the top of the backswing you will probably cast the club at the start of the downswing. Rhythm, control, consistency and even distance will be lost.

Much of the backswing depends on the address. Executing it requires little or no thought. If you have set-up properly and started the backswing correctly you are well on your way to success. You have eliminated the source of about 95 percent of all the errors made in a golf swing.

The movement back of the hips. Note by the arrow that the hips don't start to turn immediately. They make a rotation only after the weight has been shifted to the right side, and the hips never turn as far around • as do the shoulders.

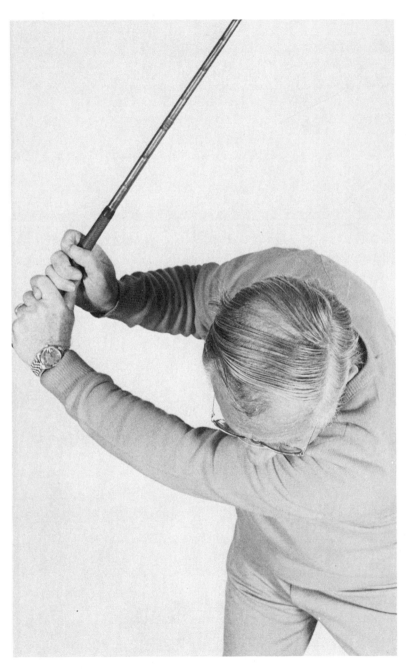

Position at the top of the backswing.

6

The Downswing

Discipline the downswing, by driving the hips through the ball, perfecting the right-leg push-off and keeping the head on the ball.

The downswing, the third and final part of the golf swing is generally considered the most important part of the process. This feeling arises because it is during this phase that the ball is hit and because so much attention has been directed at the downswing. We hear discussions about "high finish," low follow-through and head position. High speed motion picture films have been used to study wrist action through the ball and the so called "delay hit."

I couldn't even guess at the number of players who have come to me for help with what they believed were downswing problems. A few even seemed disappointed when I commented instead on their set-ups. Besides the fact that many of them were certain about the downswing being the culprit they had to correct, some players even felt they could make quick changes during their downswings in order to correct a previous fault. They may have felt, for example, that because something went wrong on their backswing, they were now going to remedy that alleged error in their downswing.

How well I remember a friend who did indeed have quick reflexes and tried to over-plan every shot on the course. On holes where a slice could only get him trouble, he carefully set himself up to draw the ball. That was good, solid strategy. However, instead of trusting his set-up, he often tried to be doubly safe by rolling his wrists into the shot. All this did was create a duck hook that frequently put him into even worse trouble than if he had hit a slice in the first place.

There simply is no time during the golf swing itself to analyze the backswing component and then alter the downswing component accordingly. Here is another place where the older player can potentially surpass a younger player. Younger people have a tendency to be impulsive. By the time we get a little older, many of us have been able to suppress that tendency.

As an older player, therefore, you can add a dimension to your game by injecting more discipline into your thinking. Learn to concentrate only on those things that will help your game. Eliminate worry and doubt from your mind. Concentrate on those moves that are important and develop a philosophy of "allowing the swing to happen." Concentrate on rhythm and smoothness, and your game will surely improve.

By the time the downswing begins, nearly every move is already determined. Too much thought at that point will only confuse and clutter your mind. You can concentrate best if you have only a small number of things to think about. An example of what I consider an unproductive thought at this point is the arc of the swing. The theory here is that the downswing arc is closer to the body than the backswing arc. This is correct, but it happens as a result of key moves—and need not be consciously attempted. Delayed hand action also is automatic, meaning that any conscious attempt to delay the hit will ruin the swing. With very few exceptions, what happens in the downswing is the result of what happened earlier in the swing. Let me point out, too, that the finish of the swing, whether high or low, has nothing to do with the ball. The ball is long gone by the time the swing is finished. The only thing that the finish position can tell you is what you might have done earlier. I would rather concentrate solely on those earlier moves.

What exactly does happen on the downswing? The first thing that happens is that some of the weight transfers back to the left side. The left foot returns to the ground and the hips begin to make a sliding move back to the left. This means that a golfer has two motions taking place in opposite directions at the same time. The weight of the club head is still moving back (or to the right) while the weight of the lower body has begun to move forward (or to the left). It is that forward sliding motion that begins before the club head is all the way back that gives power to the swing and automatically delays the hit through the ball. It is very important to emphasize that the hips return to the left with a sliding motion—not a turning motion—at the start of the downswing. If they did turn, or rotate, they would throw the club to the outside of the body (or push thyclub away from the body), and the dreadful outside-in swing would result. The sliding motion of the hips also provides more power through the ball than would be the case with a turning motion. Finally, the fact that the hips are parallel to the ball with a slide motion provides more opportunity to make square contact between the club head and the ball. The older player needs to be sure

his hips drive through the ball. There is a tendency to slow body movement with age and the older player needs to work against this trend. It
will increase his power and accuracy if he can do so.

After the hips have moved through the ball, they do make a slight
turn to the left. The hips thus are out of the way and it is possible for
the player to hit solidly through the ball. The transfer of weight to the
left side has moved the shoulders, arms and hands into the hitting position and momentum completes the finish. These movements will produce a good result provided that the head has remained on the ball.
That means the head must not move past the ball on the downswing. It
has been my experience that the one major error made by players on
the downswing is moving the head off the ball. That is about the only
part of the downswing that does not automatically take place as a result
of what happened earlier. I have seen a number of older players lunging
at the ball in an attempt to add power to their shots. In actuality they
are subtracting power. Older players need a more efficient swing and
they consequently must pay particular attention to head position on the
downswing.

There are two concepts concerning a downswing that deserves mention. One is the straight left arm. Generally, that is stressed as an important factor in the backswing, and sometimes it is mentioned as necessary
at the address position. As I've already said, I do not consider the
straight left arm vital to a good swing. In fact, it is generally undesirable
since it is not natural for most players. The ramrod straight left arm will
often cause tension in the backswing, and that is ruinous. The only time
a straight left arm becomes necessary is in the zone that begins just
prior to impact with the ball and continues for a short time immediately
following impact. However, the pulling motion caused by the weight
transfer straightens the left arm in this crucial hitting zone. So a golfer
need not worry about this ingredient as long as the swing is solid.

The other thing I hear mentioned very frequently is that looking up
from the ball ruins a shot. In plain fact though, it is very difficult to
jerk your head up on the downswing. The reason for this is the driving
momentum of the swing. That momentum is all down and through the
ball, and it is nearly impossible to jerk the head up when the whole
body is driving down. What can and often does happen, however, is that
the player moves his head *off* the ball. He may do this in two ways.
Some players move the head forward, causing any one of a variety of
errors, but chiefly causing a slice or a very high or very low shot
(depending on how far the head moved). The other head movement
some players make involves movement around the ball to the left. This
is a type of twisting, or turning motion and generally causes either a

hook or a very low (even topped) shot. The way to avoid both of these errors is to practice keeping the head over the ball while hitting shots. Because this is where the head must be during every good shot, it is one characteristic that all good players share. This is not the same, however, as keeping the head down all throughout the swing. We all want to see and enjoy those beautiful shots that we hit. Stay over the ball until the right shoulder passes under the chin and lifts the head up with a natural action. This is very different from the movement that takes place as a result of anxiety. In that case you are already afraid of where the ball is going even *before* you have hit it. The head is jerked forward and off the ball in an attempt to see what is happening.

There is another downswing action that has received too much attention in various articles. That involves the action of the right shoulder when it moves down, below the left shoulder's height, just before impact with the ball. This means that the shoulders are not level at the time the ball is struck. I have seen many players consciously try to execute this action, usually by dipping the right shoulder as they come into the ball. Such a conscious effort is a mistake, however, for the same reason that a conscious effort to delay the action of the hand is a mistake: both actions will automatically take place if the preceding components of the swing have gone according to play, and making a conscious effort to achieve what should be natural will very likely lead to other errors. The right shoulder drops because the hips have moved out from under the upper body due to their sliding motion. If the hips had instead rotated during the downswing, the shoulders would have remained level. My main point is that a steady head and the push-off from the right foot at the start of the downswing produce the slide—and that the slide, in turn, enforces a lowered right shoulder. To make any conscious attempt to drop the right shoulder, on the other hand, will probably lead to hitting behind the ball. It is obvious, therefore, that the golfer who has started his swing properly doesn't have to worry about dropping his left shoulder. That lowered right shoulder automatically happens and gives the player a downward stroke through the ball. The exception is driving, because in that stroke the player doesn't want to hit *down* with the driver. But even there the player makes an adjustment at the beginning (playing the ball well forward) to give himself an ascending type of swing. The reason for doing this is to eliminate any possible backspin in the drive.

In any golfing shot the player must move all the way through the ball. He must finish his swing. Using correct terminology, the player moves back to the right on the backswing and then all the way through the ball to the left on the downswing. If he stops the movement of the body through the ball, he is in danger of slapping at the ball with his hands, ruining the shot.

Another question that is often raised concerns the respective power of the hands at the time of the hit. "Do I actually hit the ball with my right hand?" is a question I am often asked. This query I always answer with a most emphatic *yes*, because it is with the right hand that a person (a right-handed person, of course) generates his power. Ask yourself how hard a blow you could produce by a backhand motion of your left hand. Wouldn't that blow be much weaker than a blow struck with your right hand, using a type of slapping or forehand motion? The answer seems obvious. It should also be mentioned that your left hand starts from a position closer to the ball than does your right hand. If the two hands work at the same speed, the club face must be open at impact since the right hand will be behind the left hand at the time of contact with the ball. Now it is true that we do not want the right hand to overpower the left hand: we desire a firm left hand and wrist all the way through the ball. That left hand must be the guiding hand through the ball; among other things, it gives us something to hit against. But it's also important to remember that we have a much stronger left hand grip because we hold the club with three fingers in the left hand as against only two in the right hand. Then, too, we hold the club close to the palm in the left hand while only with the fingers of the right hand. A golfer who finds his left wrist cupping or collapsing at impact merely has to firm the grip in the last three fingers of his left hand. He should definitely not weaken the grip in his right hand. Golf is a two-handed game and both hands must work together. A player with a firm grip at the start of the swing is unlikely to weaken it during the swing *unless* he starts the club back on the backswing with a jerky movement.

It seems worthwhile at this point to indicate how some of the things we have advocated at the address and at the start of the backswing affect the downswing. The natural and relaxed set-up keeps tension out of the swing as a whole. Tension in the backswing, for example, usually causes a player to jump at the ball on the downswing. Picking up the club on the backswing usually causes him to cast at the ball on the downswing. The right hand passing the left usually produces a bad shot. If the backswing is not a one-piece affair, the player will not come into the ball with the sequence of moving parts that I have outlined. Finally, if the hips turn too far on the backswing, or if the weight goes to the outside of the right leg, or if the knees are locked, the player will not be able to shift his weight quickly back to the left side at the start of the downswing. A key move on the downswing is the push-off from the right leg. That move causes the hips to slide to the left and adds both power and accuracy. This is vital for the older player since he needs all the leg action he can generate to make up for any loss of strength with age.

It is my sincere hope that all of this discussion will cause the reader to conclude that the downswing is very uncomplicated. I also hope that I have made my point about there being nothing to think about. You have already done the needed thinking when you set-up to the ball and when you begin your backswing. If you want to work at something as far as the backswing is concerned, work on the steady head position. There is very little else that you can do as far as mechanics are concerned to improve your downswing.

There are a couple of psychological things that can help, however. One is to avoid trying to steer the ball. Time and time again I have seen a player face a difficult shot that he decides he wants to play safe. He may shorten his swing, slow down his usual tempo and just punch the ball toward safety. Chances are that the ball will never reach its intended target for the player has unwisely introduced many new sources of error. The very fact that he has changed his tempo means that he is calling upon a swing that he seldom uses. It would be much wiser to stay with that which is well grooved. Slowing down may well mean that you have slowed down only one part of the swing—and that part usually involves the body. This is a grievous error because, with age, body action usually slows somewhat anyway and you don't want it any slower. Slow body movement allows the hands to take over, usually causing a very loose, flippy type of hitting action. Then, too, when you try just to poke the ball somewhere you are not likely to swing the club—another grievous error. If you face a difficult shot be sure that you set-up and begin the swing properly. You may wish to firm up your grip a little but anything else only adds the chance of error.

Finally, and perhaps most important, try to think positively. Learn to have confidence in your swing and try to remove negative thoughts from your mind. If you worry about that trap on the left you are likely to move off the ball and your shot will probably head toward that trap. Any kind of anxiety will cause tension and the swing will not produce the desired result. Outside of a steady head there is little that can be done on the downswing to facilitate a good swing. There is much that can be done to ruin it. It is most difficult for example, to move all the way through your shot if you tense up. *I firmly believe that a good set-up, an initially correct backswing move, and a steady head almost guarantee a good shot.* No one hits them perfectly every time; but if you will relax, develop confidence and trust your swing, you will show steady improvement.

Note that the first move at the start of the downswing is a shifting of the weight back to the left foot. The hips begin their move back to the left. It is this move that supplies the power for the hitting action through the ball by automatically delaying the hand action.

The hips slide (rather than turn) at the start of the downswing and this move causes a rapid weight transfer.

A

Note here the importance of the sliding action of the hips. Pay particular attention in this sequence to the delayed action due to the sliding hip action and the movement of the legs.

B

C

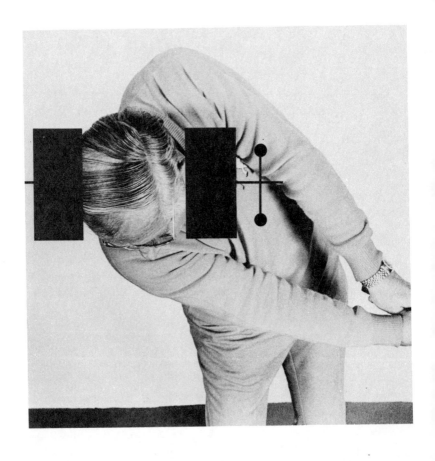

A steady head position is the only mechanical part of a downswing which can be worked on — other movement is automatic.

7

Beginning Golf
After 45

Make a great beginning, with realistic goals, natural posture and rhythm — not power.

Frequently, when one golfer plays well, other less skilled players ask him at what age he first began playing. If the answer is that he began early in life the questioner generally replies that he suspected such would be the case. The tacit assumption is that to play well one *must* begin playing when he is very young. We have all heard in a variety of ways about not being able to teach an old dog new tricks. The underlying idea seems to be that the coordination required to become a skilled golfer can come only from early exposure to the game.

There are two important points here. On the one hand, I do not wish to suggest that it is not an asset to have started golf at a young age. If the swing is properly developed it can become grooved early in life and it should be possible to maintain it with some regular play. Any skill developed early in life provides something to fall back on. It forms a solid base and even if not used for a time it is easy to rekindle.

An equally important point, however, is that early exposure to the game is not vital to later development of skill. The only option not open to a player who takes up golf later in life is the option of becoming a professional, because a successful professional golf career must begin fairly early in life. But a skilled golf game at the non-professional level can indeed be developed later in life. Golf is primarily a mental game. It is not a game that demands a heavily muscled body. Since the human mind does not lose its capacity to learn, golf skill can be attained late in life. Several recent excellent examples of this have been reported in *Golf World Magazine*. A 1976 issue included this: "Ed Lipscombe scored 62 at Hampton (Va.) G.C., 5,578 — yarder of par 70. Par was reduced by one due to green repair at one hole. He bettered his age by one shot with six birdies, one eagle and one bogey." Quite an achievement, but how about this one? A. H. Berghold scored 38-43-81 on the south course at Lake Hefner, Oklahoma City, six days prior to his 83rd birthday. He *began* playing the game at age 70 *(Golf World,* October 1, 1976).

These are fine illustrations of starting and playing golf late and well, but I have seen many, many more during my years as a teaching professional. Late starters are generally men who have worked hard most of their lives. They had little time for anything but work, and then one day they decided to take life a little easier. Unfortunately, many of these men approach golf just as they did their business careers. They work hard at the game but, unlike business, it doesn't develop properly. Soon they become discouraged and the clubs become used with less frequency. I want to help the reader develop a plan of attack that will change that whole picture around.

We can go far toward success if we make a good beginning. I believe the first step should be that of setting some realistic personal goals. What is a golfer trying to do? Does he want merely to keep the ball in play, or is score of great importance? How often will he probably be able to play, and how much does he enjoy practice? Is he a systematic person who probably will want to analyze his swing at great length? Does competition interest him, and how well does he finally want to be able to play?

These questions are exceedingly important because when answered they tell a person what his goals are in the game. If you are only able to play once or twice a week, for example, it is likely that your game will not develop as rapidly as it would were you to play three or four times weekly. Above all, though, do not push yourself. Don't try to make up for what you have missed all those years by suddenly driving yourself to develop a strong game overnight. Pace yourself and enjoy yourself. Set goals that are realistic, or else you will never know the reward of pride of accomplishment.

I believe a good second step would be to keep two ideas in mind. You want to feel comfortable as you stand up to the ball. This means that you carefully go over the chapters on the grip and the set-up. Find those positions that feel the best to you. If you find, for example, that with the advancing years you stoop a little more, accept that. Don't try to imitate the young tour player who is limber and perhaps stands more erect. You will note that I stress naturalness all through this book. I will tell you over and over that if you do not feel comfortable at the start you won't produce a good swing. Always go with what you have to work with; the result will be much better.

Secondly, you must accept the fact *you* will not hit that ball; the club does that. And it will not do it correctly if you don't swing it correctly. Try to hit the ball and you will merely throw your hands at the ball. This is a bad move for anyone but as you grow older your body action slows somewhat. If you are just now taking up the game, chances are that your body will at first move a bit more slowly compared to your hands. Along with this, think rhythm—not power. If you develop rhythm you will attain your maximum power with the least effort. That is your goal. Work to smooth out those movements.

You will notice that I have been talking about a mental attitude before saying anything about the backswing or the downswing. That is because I want you to get yourself set mentally even before you walk to the practice tee. By thinking of a few important things before you get ready to swing the club you put yourself in the right frame of mind. Mental planning goes far toward physical actualization.

Now, back to that set-up. Try out a variety of grips and select the one that feels good to you. Swing the club a number of times using your chosen grip. It would be most helpful to grip and regrip the club numerous times in order to get used to the feel of the club in your hands. Then go on to the set-up. Follow those procedures that were mentioned in the chapter until you feel comfortable. Always work on only one idea at a time. Keep the game simple. For example, start with a grip, then a stance with the feet, then an arm and shoulder position. Practice that procedure until it feels comfortable and seems consistent. You can use a variety of checkpoints (such as where the weight is, whether the knees remain bent, and whether your arms hang freely from your shoulders). I feel that this should be done at the practice tee. It is most difficult to get repetition if you start right out on the golf course.

Next, go to the backswing and take that one step at a time. Work on rhythm and the one-unit backswing. Do not try to think of every move that is taking place. Do the same with the downswing. You might work on the head position one time and weight transfer the next. Mainly, though, work on the mental approach. Swing the club: don't try to smash the ball out of sight.

Try to make some visits to the practice range, mainly because you will have a better chance there to develop some sort of groove for your swing. On the golf course you hit one shot and then there is a time interval before you hit the next. On the practice range you can work toward a repeating type of swing. However, practice hitting shots only as long as you enjoy doing it. When it becomes a chore, discontinue it, because after that point you will force yourself into a negative attitude and a bad swing. If at all possible try to have a brief warm-up session on the practice range before each round. After all, even professional football players warm up before a game—and they are in excellent physical condition. That *gradual* loosening up is better for the body, too.

On the course, work to keep the ball in play and always go with your percentage shot. Expect to hit some bad shots and accept them when you do. Getting angry about a bad shot will only ruin your game and your enjoyment. Set your goal as far as score is concerned according to what is reasonable for you. If you are just beginning the game it will be meaningless to your game that par is actually 72. Make up your own par and set goals for yourself that can be reached. A first goal might be, for example, to break 60—for nine holes. Once accomplished you can make your par 100. In this manner you always have something to shoot for and you avoid discouragement. However, while on the golf course do not make dramatic swing changes. Stick with your game plan and work out basic changes on the practice tee.

Three other points need to be made. An important one is learning to follow your ball. You can't rely on caddies, and fellow players will not enjoy constant countrywide ball searches. Secondly, you might be wise to consider some professional lessons. After all, you can't see your own swing; you may be moving your head off the ball unknowingly, for example. Lastly, use any gimmick you can that will aid relaxation and develop rhythm. Accept the mental challenge of the game and use the discipline that can come with age. And, yes, a little practice wouldn't hurt either; but only to the point that it is pleasant. If you hate practice sessions you will merely have to accept the fact your progress will be somewhat slower. Above all, have fun. Golf is a wonderful game and it is great just to be alive and out on that course!

8

Don't Worry About Those Sand Shots

Learn successful sand shots, with smooth rhythm, a one-piece backswing and mental discipline.

In all probability there is no part of the game that is as frightening to the average player as shots from sand. I have observed quite a number of players who approach the game with confidence until they have to step into the sand trap. Suddenly they look like different people. Tension wracks their faces and you just know by looking at them that they are going to miss that bunker shot. I have heard such negative comments as, "Oh no, there goes my whole game!"

What is more, I have even seen the sand trap sap a player's confidence even before his ball is in the trap. It's as if the very presence of the trap, quietly lying there in front of the green, poses some sort of monstrous threat. The player fails to notice anything but the trap, and his whole game plan is abandoned. Suddenly he has to "steer" his shot away from the trap, and he frequently finds himself in far more serious trouble than landing in the trap. And very often too, his negative thinking causes him to do that which he most fears—hitting right into the sand trap.

My co-author, Bud Gunn, is generally a good short iron player, but there was an occasion several years ago when he complained that he could not even hit the green with these shots. When we ventured out onto the course I found that his complaint was partially correct. He was missing the green but only when it was heavily trapped. Bud hit fine shots when the green was not guarded by sand. Further conversation divulged that he was also having trouble with sand shots. After we worked on the techniques of hitting out of traps, his short iron game returned to its previous level of proficiency.

The older player needs to come to grips with his fear of sand shots. First of all, if he does not hit the ball as far as he once could, he will find that he is coming up short on some of those very long par four holes. Generally there will be a trap or two guarding these holes and short, therefore, means in the bunker. What is more, it is generally the short cut to the green that is most heavily trapped. Another point is that the golfer who doesn't play and practice quite as often as he once did will be a little less accurate—and as a result is likely to visit more traps.

Worry about trap shots can, as I have said, adversely affect approach shots. However, the opposite is also true. The player who feels secure hitting sand shots is likely to hit better approach shots and stay out of the sand. The average golfer can prove this axiom to himself by thinking back to the day he hit a few bad trap shots near the beginning of his round. I will bet that he then found himself in many more traps the rest of the way.

There are two very positive factors in all of this, however. One is that as our skill with sand shots improves we are less likely to be called upon to display that skill. The second is that there is no reason why the older player cannot become an excellent sand player. Strength is not a necessary ingredient. Knowledge, mental discipline, and rhythm are. Where the younger person tends to be quick and impulsive, the older person is more likely to be slow and deliberate. That is exactly what is needed for success in sand. If you learn the techniques that will be provided here—and work on positive thinking—you can succeed. And you will find that sand shots are easy. Since the most commonly used of the three basic sand shots is the explosion shot, let's start with that variety.

Short Explosion Shot

We talk here about a shot that causes the ball to be moved as a result of the movement of sand that lies beneath the ball. The ball itself does not actually come in contact with the face of the club. Instead, sand is moved and the moving sand, in turn, moves the ball. The short explosion shot works differently for three different relationships of ball position and condition of sand—where the ball rests up on the sand, where the ball is in wet sand, and where the ball is buried in sand.

The set-up for a regular sand shot. Note that the ball is played well forward in the stance, the club face is wide open, and the stance is open. The successful player is relaxed with this shot, uses a slow motion tempo, and hits through the shot.

Ball rests high on sand. In this situation the ball has not sunk into the sand, and the sand is smooth around the ball—there are no hills of sand in front of or behind the ball.

Set-Up: The grip is similar to that employed with most other shots; that is, the grip is firm between the last three fingers of the left hand and between the thumb and index finger of the right hand. Arms hang naturally from the shoulders, the stance is rather narrow, and the ball is played off the left heel. The two major changes from most other shots are that the club face is decidedly open, and that the stance is very open.

There are important reasons for the open club face and open stance. Look at the typical sand wedge and you will find a heavy flange on the bottom. The purpose of this flange is to keep the club head from digging too deeply into the sand, thus stopping the movement of the sand and therefore the ball. The ball will then go only a few feet if the club head digs too deeply. The open club face acts like a razor blade and easily cuts through the sand. This provides easy movement through the shot and the ball flies out of the trap with little effort.

The open stance causes a more upright backswing and thereby allows a natural digging action. We do not want to sweep into the shot as is done with a driver, for example. The open stance automatically produces a sufficient downward movement of the club face, similar to that employed with a wedge shot from the fairway.

The final preparation is to dig the feet into the sand. This not only gives the player a solid base, but in addition allows him to test the composition of the sand. It is important to know whether there is a thin layer of sand, whether it is wet below the surface or whether it is soft and powdery.

Stroke: Like any stroke in golf, it is important with the sand shot to have a one-piece backswing and smooth rhythm. There is one added imperative with the sand shot, and that is a slow swing. This is because we want the club face to hit about two inches behind the ball and slice through the sand. If the club face comes bouncing into the shot there is great danger of skulling or bouncing the club head into the shot. The slow motion swing brings the club face gently to the ball, not bouncing into the back of the ball. As with other shots the head remains over the ball to insure that the bottom of the arc will be just behind the ball.

Distance: With shorter shots the backswing is slightly shorter, but it should never be so short that the player jumps at the ball. With longer shots the legs drive into the shot more. A player should never try to speed up his hands or he will lose the slow motion effect. With the open club face technique he can always aim about two inches behind the ball, regardless of the length of the shot. The player must also keep moving through the shot: If his swing stops, the sand stops; and so does the ball...it doesn't clear the trap. A sand shot is a very delicate stroke. Most of us mistakenly try to use brawn. Trap play, done with ease, can be very simple.

Ball rests in wet sand. The ball tends to fly out of wet sand with greater velocity, and as a result the force of the whole swing should be reduced. That means less drive with the legs and slightly slower tempo. Those are the only changes recommended since the open club face allows the club to cut through the sand.

Ball buried in sand. There are occasions when the ball is partly embedded in the sand. Generally this happens when a high shot falls directly into a bunker with soft, dry sand. The buried lie has been called a fried egg because the ball resembles the yolk, and the ridges around the ball become like the egg white. Literally, the whole fried egg must be lifted onto the green. There are two main methods of doing that—with an open club face or with a square club face.

I still recommend the open club face as the best sand shot even when the ball is buried. The edge of the club will cut through the sand and lift the ball out with little effort. The golfer moves the point of club impact back, behind the last ridge; or, in other words, several more inches behind the ball than he would otherwise be aiming at. We do not want the club face to dig too deeply into the sand, because that will stop the club head. Aim left of the hole and use the same stroke as described earlier. If the ball is deeply buried, a player may wish to make his swing even more upright than the open stance that I recommend would make it. To do this, he can lift his arms a little more quickly on the backswing than he does with other shots. The latter would be an exceptional technique to use, again, since the open stance already provides a more upright swing. A driving motion of the legs provides the power needed to move the sand and the ball. A player should not try to speed up his swing, and do not try to dig the ball out with hand power. The set-up will make it all happen very naturally.

The second way to hit a buried ball is with a square club face, and some fine players use this because they feel it can dig the ball out better. In this case, the arms must be lifted more abruptly on the backswing and the club head struck closer to the ball than the open face requires. The slow motion swing is still used, as is the open stance and the driving action of the legs. If this method works well for a golfer, he should use it, but he should also allow for more run on the ball after it hits the green. I prefer the open club face, but no one method works best for everyone.

Chip Shot

This second basic variety of the sand shot, chipping, works only when the ball rests high on the sand—and is generally used when the ball is a long way from the pin. The type of terrain determines the club used. If the player has to come over a lip on the trap, you would use a more lofted club, such as a 9-iron or wedge. A flat trap and level green would allow a chip shot with a less lofted club, such as a 7-iron. Of particular importance, too, is the distance from the hole; a less lofted club generally causes the ball to roll more than a lofted club.

Grip is essentially the same one used in other golf shots; stance is also the same one used in other chip shots. The ball is played off the right heel. The stroke itself is the same as a regular chip shot stroke, but one must be especially careful not to hit behind the ball since the sand will then stop the club head. *(Where* the club head strikes is a great difference between the chip and explosion sand shots.) The player must therefore be more steady on the chip out of sand because there is less margin for error than with other chip shots. However, if he moves through the shot and keeps a steady head, the chances for success are great. One other piece of advice: always remember that with hard packed or wet sand, the ball will come out much faster.

Long Shot out of Sand

The third basic sand shot, besides exploding and chipping, amounts to a full iron shot with a few minor adjustments. The major difference between a long shot out of sand and an equivalently long shot off grass is that the former doesn't allow hitting sharply down on the ball—because in so doing the club head may be stopped by the sand. However, I believe that once again the proper set-up will go far toward guaranteeing a good shot.

My advice to the reader about long shots out of sand consists of eight steps to follow.

1. Plant your feet very solidly into the sand. This will tell you something about the consistency of the sand and also prevent you from slipping.

2. Since you cannot sole the club in the sand, hold it several inches above the sand. This will help prevent a sweep into the ball. Remember,

The set-up for a chip shot out of the sand trap. The set-up and swing are similar to a regular chip shot. Hit down and through the ball. This shot works best when the ball is sitting up and when you don't have to hit over an obstacle to get to the green. The ball will come out low and run for a fairly long distance.

The top of the backswing for an explosion shot. Notice the upright swing, which lets the player dig under the ball more easily to lift it into the air quickly. This upright swing is automatic because of the very open stance.

you want to pick the ball out of the sand; holding the club above the sand at address automatically sets up that type of action.

3. Use a slightly open stance. This produces a more upright swing and therefore helps pick the ball clean from the sand.

4. Use the same tempo as with a regular iron shot, and in particular never rush at the ball. Use a smooth swing or you will increase the potential for error.

5. The head must remain absolutely still. This is always important; it is doubly so when hitting a long shot out of sand. Head movement can change your swing plain, causing you to hit either behind the ball or to scoop sand in front of the ball.

6. Use the same general grip and swing as with other shots. Stay relaxed; your set-up will take care of the fact that the ball lies on sand rather than grass. Trust your swing and the shot will not prove difficult.

7. Be sure you have sufficient loft to clear the lip. Often in an attempt to gain distance players select clubs with little loft, only to find that they then hit the lip of the trap and lose everything. You can open the club face *slightly* in order to get the ball into the air more quickly. In that case aim slightly left of your target and just take a regular swing. The ball will rise into the air more quickly and yet you will gain greater distance than if you had used a more lofted club.

8. Work on your mental attitude. Age is not a handicap with sand play; be confident and smooth. That ball will come out of the sand without the use of brute strength.

9

The Importance of Chipping

Lower your scores by using a firm grip and judging distance on chip shots.

Certain golf shots must be executed with a high degree of finesse. They require little or no power, and yet they are crucial if the player is to lower his score. One of these shots, the chip, is especially vital because skill in this department allows a player to salvage par even when he's missed a green. This is particularly important for the high handicapper and the older player. As a player loses some of his power he will find that he *can* master it. This is one of several parts of the game that do not involve power so it's made to order for the older player. Like good wine, chipping should only improve with age.

Another reason why the older player should master the chip shot is that he *can* master it. This is one of the several parts of the game that do not involve power so it's made to order for the older player. Like good wine, chipping should only improve with age.

It is important to know exactly what a chip shot is and what it can accomplish. Chipping generally involves a low shot that lands on the green and runs toward the cup. This is not a universal description, because there are occasions when the ball must land just off the edge of the green in order to have any chance of stopping by the cup. Generally, through, the ball should land on the green because otherwise it is difficult to judge how it will probably respond. Greens are usually smooth, while collars of greens are often bumpy and quite often have long grass.

Occasional variations to this type of shot include higher shots that are meant to negotiate some obstacle, such as a small bunker. In that case a more lofted club will be selected in order to carry the ball over the bunker and then allow it to run to the hole. The distinction is between the chip, or low shot and the pitch, a higher shot. With the pitch shot we use a more lofted club and expect the ball to run less after it hits the green, while with the chip shot we intend to hit the ball lower and to allow it to run more once it reaches the green. A common chipping club used from just off the edge of the green is a six-iron. A common pitching club is a highly lofted club such as a wedge. The wedge can also be used for a chip shot, however; there, it is played in such a manner that the ball is hit on a lower arc than would be· the case if one were hitting a pitch shot. It is vital that in hitting a proper chip shot the ball must be struck with a *descending* blow by the club head. If the club head strikes the ball while moving upward, or ascending, it puts loft on the ball—and the player does not know whether it will hit a soft spot in the green and stop, or hit a hard spot on the green and continue to run. A prime objective of the chip shot is to impart over-spin, and this overspin produces a consistent roll to the ball. Consistency in chipping is extremely important: putting backspin on one shot and overspin on the next will prevent a golfer from judging how hard a hit is needed to get the ball to the hole. A number of factors work together in hitting a chip shot with a descending blow, and these are covered in the description below.

Grip

The grip used when hitting chip shots is essentially the same as the one used in most other golf shots. It starts with the last three fingers of the left hand firmly gripping the club. The little finger of the right hand overlaps the index finger of the left hand, in the Vardon grip, and the thumb and index finger of the right hand grip the club firmly. As with most other golf shots, the thumb and index fingers of the right hand serve as the feelers, enabling a golfer to determine how firmly to hit the shot. Firmness with the last three fingers of the left hand increases the chances of hitting through the shot—and cuts down the possibility of hitting behind the ball, scooping the shot, or even topping it. Firmness is especially important for the older player because looseness will tend to cause jerkiness. This will mean a loss of rhythm.

The set-up position for the chip shot involves an open stance, natural arm position and hands that are ahead of the ball. The chip shot helps the golfer to keep a consistent roll to the ball.

Quite some time ago an older player asked me to take a look at his chipping style. He reported that he had no consistency with these shots and when I watched him hit a few I could readily see why. It seems he had read somewhere that a "very light grip" would mean greater feel. Unfortunately, his grip was so loose that he lost control of the club. As a result, his wrist action was flippy through the ball and this in turn caused much nervousness whenever he approached this most delicate shot.

Set-up

The stance used for the chip shot is considerably open, with the left foot drawn well back of the intended line and well back of the right foot the right foot remains square to the line, and the weight is slightly favoring the left foot. This enables a player to move his left hip through the chip shot, keeping his body ahead of the shot and thus insuring that the ball is struck with a descending blow. The knees are slightly flexed to allow fluidity of movement. Any tendency to lock the knees will restrict a player's movement through the ball, causing bad shots. As usual, the arms hang from the shoulders in a comfortable, relaxed position, and the golfer is positioned closer to the ball than in other golf shots. This is the case because the clubs used are shorter clubs and because the desired tendency is to grip farther down on the shaft for greater control. The ball is positioned in the middle of the stance for the typical chip shot, and the hands are placed well ahead of the ball—two more positioning techniques that work toward hitting the ball on a descending stroke. With the hands placed ahead of the ball, the tendency to hit behind the ball and scoop it is reduced.

Stroke

Good golfers use either of two stroke variations in hitting chip shots. Both variations involve different usages of the wrists, arms, and shoulders. One variety, the stiff-wristed approach, has the club carried back on the backswing with little wrist break—it's primarily a movement of the arms and shoulders in a one-unit move. As a result, very little wrist action is used on the backswing. The second variety employs a quicker wrist break, more usage of the wrists, and less movement of the arms and shoulders. Some excellent chippers use the first of these approaches and others use the second. The individual golfer should experiment in order to determine which approach works better for him.

Whichever chip shot stroke is used, very few good chippers use a wristy downswing and a scooping action in hitting the ball. In other words, those who use a quick wrist break on the backswing normally hit against a firm left hand on the downswing so they do not flip the right hand over the left. Those who use an arm stroke on the backswing also hit against a firm left hand, and thus the downswing of both approaches is quite similar. At no point should a chip shot be wristy—or else the player will probably top or hit behind the ball. Again, the right hand, particularly the thumb and index finger, applies the force to the chip shot and also provides a sense of feel. Because an older player's nerves tend to be less steady than a younger person's, I recommend the arm-stroke chip shot for older players. This shot makes sense for an older player, especially because it has fewer moving parts than the other chip shot variety.

The leg action with the chip shot is strikingly similar to the leg action in most golf shots—the main difference is the reduced magnitude of leg action that a short chip shot requires. The legs must remain loose, and the knees relaxed throughout the swing because any tension will restrict movement through the ball. There is a slight movement of the hips through the ball so that the left hip can get out of the way on the downswing and allow for hitting the ball on the downswing. If the left hip locks, the club head will come into the ball in an ascending manner and cause inconsistent hitting from one shot to the next. Some leg action helps prevent this locked-hip condition from happening because it helps the hips move successfully through the shot. The chipping stroke itself should be a short, crisp shot that imparts a consistent overspin to the ball.

Variations

Occasionally, a ball will come to rest in the spongy grass around the green or in heavy rough. A variation of the usual chip shot is called for in this case: a very firm, short "jab stroke." This is a very firm, short hit to the ball, with very little intended followthrough. The purpose of this is to pop the ball out of the rough very quickly; a smooth follow-through is generally not possible.

Occasionally, the chip shot can be played in a slightly higher type of arc, but overspin is still desired for the ball. In such a case, the ball can be moved slightly more forward in the stance (closer to the left foot), and the same stroke applied. However, generally speaking, it is better to simply go to a club with more loft and to use the same type of stroke.

A lot of chipping practice is needed to develop judgment about the clubs that consistently produce the best results. A few suggestions, however, can be made. For chipping uphill, when the ball lies just off the green, a club with less loft—such as a five- or six-iron—is usually best. The main idea with the chip shot is to get the ball to the green and then let it roll. So if there's a long way to go to the cup, a club with less loft is best. For chipping downhill, however, a club with more loft is used, such as an eight- or nine-iron. The farther a player is from the green, the greater the club loft he should use—so that there will be enough loft to get the ball to the edge of the green and then allow it to run to the hole. Occasionally, a green is tiered, with one section lying well above or well below another section. This requires anticipating where on the green the ball will land and how much farther from that point the overspin will probably take the ball. A ball hit into a hill, of course, will stop rather abruptly. The golfer must decide ahead of time whether he will hit the ball short of the sharp hill and allow it to run up the bank of the hill to the pin, or whether he will carry it over the elevated portion and allow it to run toward the hole. To have the ball land on the green short of the hill, a club with limited loft is used; to carry the hill and allow the ball to run toward the hole, a higher loft club such as a nine-iron or a wedge is in order.

The type of stroke used is important to the success of the chip shot, but judgment about where on the green to aim for and about club loft is at least as important as the shot itself. If a player works on his judgment he should find that he can become very skilled around the greens and that his scores will drop.

One example of what you can accomplish in the thinking department involves checking your line to the hole. Suppose the green slopes from left to right. If you start your ball to the left of the hole you can allow it to "die" gradually into the hole. You will find that judgment of distance becomes easier. On the other hand, had you played the ball right at the hole you would need perfect touch to get it near the hole. If you hit even a little too hard, the hill will cause the ball to gather momentum immediately and it may roll a considerable distance away. Always note, too, where you want the ball to be to make your putt as easy as possible. So along with practicing chip shots, practice and experiment with the judgment—making part of your short game around the greens. Don't rush your shots; plan them out and be deliberate. Skill with the chip shot can often make up for yards lost with the driver. Since you have lost the brashness of youth, learn to rely upon the wisdom of age.

10

The Value
of the Wedge

*Save strokes on the green, by using
the sand wedge for pitching, planning your moves and staying down
on the shot.*

There are very few clubs that have as much dramatic impact on golf as
the wedge. The wedge is an exceedingly important club to players of all
different levels of skill. The high handicapper is generally a player who
does not hit many greens in regulation. As a result he needs skill with
the wedge in order to save par. The low handicapper who uses the
wedge successfully will find that he is not only saving pars but also
recording more birdies. In addition, as you find you have a better short
game you tend to relax more with your approach shots. This usually
will mean that you hit better approach shots.

Skill with the wedge is a must for the older player. As he loses
yardage off the tee he will not be able to reach some of the longer holes
with his approach shot. In order to reduce his handicap he needs to be
able to place his wedge shots near the pin. Fortunately, there is nothing
to prevent an older golfer from becoming an excellent wedge player.
This is another one of those parts of golf that do not require strength or
power. In fact, I believe very often those who are power-oriented have
trouble mastering the wedge. Finesse is often ignored by a power golfer.
He has often been too successful for his own good in muscling shots,
and, that approach won't produce good results with the wedge. Consequently, some players actually improve their golf games when they lose
raw power. They develop that rhythm, touch, and technique that is so
important with the wedge.

I once worked with a man in his late 50's who hated to admit that he had lost some of his muscle power. He constantly put every ounce of raw power he possessed into each shot that he hit. One could literally hear him grunt as he hit the ball. Naturally, he had problems in every part of his game; but his wedge shots were especially bad.

I worked many hours with him on his wedge shots and gradually convinced him that rhythm and finesse were vital. An interesting sidelight was that as he changed his approach with the wedge he also altered his technique with other parts of the game. His whole golf game improved as the carryover from the wedge took place. He is now a fine wedge player, but the rest of his game has dramatically improved, too.

There are, of course, two clubs in the bag called wedges. One is a pitching wedge and the other is a sand wedge. The sand wedge is the most lofted, heaviest, and yet shortest club in the bag. It will not get the distance of a pitching wedge, but it is the club that I recommend for those short, high shots to the green. Properly used, it will provide high loft and great backspin on balls hit to the green. Since it has a rounded flange it will slide over the turf rather than digging into the ground as does the pitching wedge. I do advise use of the pitching wedge when the ball lies on bare ground. The reason for this is because with the wide flange, the sand wedge prevents a player from getting under the ball. The sharper flange on the pitching wedge also makes that club more suitable for shots out of deep rough. It allows the club head to cut through grass that would block or slow up the sand wedge.

Unless I specify otherwise, when I speak about a wedge in this chapter, I mean the sand wedge. Golfers who have used the sand wedge only in sand have a pleasant surprise in store. They will find that pitch shots are much easier with this club and have a greater variety of shots open to them. If you learn the various shots presented here you will literally have a shot for all occasions.

The Lob Shot

This shot is a high shot that floats to the green with little backspin but, most importantly, without overspin. The shot is used when a golfer has only a short distance to negotiate and must have height to go over a trap, or when the pin is placed in the front part of the green. Even where a player can't use a big swing and thus attain a lot of backspin, the lack of overspin on the lob shot enables him to keep his ball from running far from the pin once it lands on the green. A lob shot doesn't require that the ball be sitting up high on the grass, but it can't be down in a hole either. Parts of the set-up are similar for other shots, such as a firm left-hand grip, and a firm grip with the thumb and index finger in the right hand. The stance is narrow and open as for any short iron. The ball is played forward of the middle of the stance. The swing is short and crisp with no flipping action of the right hand. The player must hit down and through the shot, and he will automatically do this as a result of his set-up. The narrow, open stance causes a more upright backswing and ball impact on the descending part of the stroke. The loft of the club lifts the ball; if the player himself tries to scoop it with his right hand, he'll ruin the shot. The movement of the hips through the ball insures the downward hit through the ball. All told, this is an easy shot as long as the player doesn't become tense and change the swing once it has begun. The two most common errors made on this shot are restriction of the hips on the downswing, preventing movement through the shot, and a wristy, flippy stroke. A firm left wrist prevents the latter from happening. The lob shot doesn't require power, but it does require rhythm. Patience is also important the shot can't be rushed.

Hitting with Backspin

It is virtually impossible to obtain significant backspin unless one hits a nearly full wedge. Backspin comes from pinching the ball against the ground and the club face. If the club is not moving rapidly at impact there will not be sufficient pinch of the ball to cause backspin. The ball will merely slide off the club face and float to the green with very little spin.

Consequently, the only way to give backspin to the ball is to hit the shot with authority. It is possible to grip down on the club (closer to the shaft) in order to secure a harder hit but less distance. But, remember that if you have a very short shot to the green you are going to get some run on the ball after it hits the green. The procedure for the wedge with backspin is similar to that used with most short iron shots. As is always the case, use a firm grip and a narrowed, open stance. The ball is played from the middle of the stance in order to hit it on the descending phase of the swing. Keep the swing short and firm, and do not use a lot of wrist action. Be particularly careful not to flip the right hand at the ball—in other words, don't scoop at the shot. If the right hand rolls over the left hand before impact, you will either hit behind the shot (the so-called "fat shot") or you will top the ball. The topped shot is particularly bad since the ball will then run like a jack-rabbit, and may well roll over the green. Always trust your swing; remember that your set-up will produce the type of action you want if you allow it to; and move through the shot. This type of wedge shot is just a miniature of the longer iron shots and it is not difficult if you relax and move freely.

The Low Wedge Shot

There are times when you will not want your wedge shot high. Maybe that shot must travel under the branches of a tree before it reaches the green. Maybe you wish to drive the ball through a wind, or you simply feel you can judge the distance better with a lower type of shot. The skilled player should be able to alter the trajectory of his shot. This low shot takes place with little variation in the set-up. The stance is still narrow and open. The ball is placed in the middle of the stance. The major variation takes place on the backswing where, after the initial take away, there is a quick wrist-break. In other words, for this low shot there is a much quicker cocking of the wrists on the backswing. On the downswing the club is swung through the ball with no wrist action at all. The arms carry the club through the ball and as a result of this action the hands are well ahead of the club. This decreases the club loft and provides a shot that travels low but still has some backspin.

The High, Short Wedge Shot

Here is a shot that can be used when the player finds himself very close to the green (within 10 yards) and in need of a high shot. To use this shot the ball must be sitting up on grass because the intent is to slide the wedge under the ball. Stance remains the same as with the other wedge shots. The major change involves placing the ball off the left toe. Then the stroke is made with little wrist action because the technique merely involves the sliding of the wedge under the ball. There is not an actual hitting action. The club face should be laid open; this makes the club slide under the ball with great ease. Tempo is very important; do not try to rush the shot. A very important ingredient is to keep moving on the shot because with the ball so far forward the player must move a long way in order to get to it. The result will be a short, very high shot that will not travel far once it hits the green.

The Slow-Motion Wedge Shot

The name of this shot is suggestive of a sand trap type shot, and that is exactly what it is. In order to be able to hit this shot the ball must be sitting up off the ground, but that condition could prevail in the rough.

Set-up for a typical wedge shot.

Set-up for a high wedge shot.

Set-up for a low wedge shot.

The ball is played off the left heel, stance is open and the same width as for a full swing from a sand trap. The club face is partly open and if the ball must be hit out of the rough, be particularly firm with the left-hand grip. This is necessary because the long grass in the rough tends to grab the club head. Without a firm grip the club is apt to slip in your hand.

The swing technique is the same as that used in the sand trap—slow and smooth. Swing all the way through the ball and the club will slide under the ball, providing quick lift. The slow movement of the club lets the ball slide gently off the face of the club. It will drop softly onto the green and although it will not have much backspin it also will not run much.

If you master these shots you will be able to save strokes around the green. Learn to think out a plan of action ahead of time. Once you have selected a plan, stick to it. Never raise your shoulders up to try to lift that ball. Stay down on the shot and let the club do the work. Use those qualities of age that will work for you; namely, self-control and judgment. Develop rhythm, self-confidence and patience. Impulsiveness will destroy timing and ruin your shot. The deliberation that age usually brings can work to your advantage. At the same time, however, don't become so slow in your shot-making that tension creeps into the swing. Always go with your normal, comfortable pace.

11

Make That Putter Work for You

Improve your putting, with a steady head over the ball, a square contact with the ball and an even stroke.

Putting is very nearly another game in itself and is one of the more controversial portions of golf. One school of thought, for example, simply claims—without presenting evidence—that good putters are born and not taught. Other people claim that the reason putting can't be improved by teaching is that there are no rules to follow, that nearly everyone uses a different putting technique. Perhaps this latter view explains why so few people have studied putting systematically.

One statement about putting that doesn't cause much argument is that it's important. The first half of the old adage "drive for show and putt for dough" doesn't really make any sense—since driving sets the stage for every other shot on a given hole—but the last half is certainly true. There's just no way to score well unless a player can putt well. After all, half the total shots in a par-72 round are assigned to the putter. We all know that we have had some low rounds *principally* because on that day we putted well.

The question comes up about what influence age has on putting. There are some people who would say that after age forty the nerves become so jumpy that good putting is not possible. I disagree with that statement, just as I disagree with the statement that a golfer can't be taught to putt well. The reason I disagree is that putting is a classic example of mind over matter, which among other things, means that good putting can't happen unless the mind expects that it *will* happen. Conversely, to expect to do poorly, to have jumpy nerves, or the "yips" has to lead to putting troubles. Any negative thoughts translate themselves into bodily tension and that ruins rhythm. An excellent example of this involves a player I know who often feels uncertain of his line on a breaking putt. He frequently jerks his head up even before impact and thereby throws his putter off the intended line. The same is true with regard to the functioning of the nervous system. If you are expecting those old nerves to jump, you will tense up and they *will* jump.

Putting does not require brute strength. Power does not play a part in the stroke. So there is no reason why an older player can't become a successful putter. In fact, if he has been playing for years, he should have learned more about reading greens, and this added knowledge should give him a putting edge on the younger player. The main problem for the older putter is going to be overcoming the idea, so often stated in our society, that age is a severe handicap. The positive mental attitude that was discussed earlier applies with special force to putting. It would probably help to look over Chapter 2 whenever you find doubt creeping into your mind about any shot, but especially putting.

I believe that 80 percent of successful putting is psychological. In an earlier book I recounted an experience that my co-author, Bud Gunn, had with hypnosis. Bud, a clinical psychologist, hypnotized a golfer who had a very poor putting stroke. For a short time the man putted superbly, even though his stroke remained as unsound as ever. His success finally ended when his poor stroke let him down, but the experience proved how far confidence alone can take a putter. A player's goal should be to develop confidence in putting based on a sound technique. The technique must include certain essential ingredients, which I will describe in a moment, but the technique must also be unusually well suited to a player's personal characteristics and comfort.

As an example of matching sound putting movements to personal comfort, I remember giving a lesson to a lady who could not even make short putts with any consistency. She told me, however, that at one time she had been a fine putter. I asked if she could recall any changes that might have taken place in her putting style. She thought for a moment and then informed me that she no longer putted with her elbows out. Someone had "corrected" her style. When I watched her putt it was obvious that she was not comfortable with her new technique. She literally moved all over the place. I suggested she go back to her old style, and the putting improved immediately.

Another example is that of the great former golfer Patty Berg. Berg's putting technique involved positioning her feet as far apart from each other as she could comfortably stand. This stance was considered highly unorthodox, but Berg was a champion for many years. Whether or not her putting technique was directly responsible, it obviously did not hurt her game, and it is a good example of matching effective putting with comfort.

Those essentials that I believe characterize all good putting include, first of all, a steady head over the ball. They also include a square contact between the putter face and the ball. Thirdly, the putting stroke must have some sort of a smooth rhythm. It is worthwhile to examine each of these ingredients in detail.

The head's steady position is important because in order to secure a square hit a player must in some manner secure the position of his body over the ball. He must not only plant his feet, but his whole body as well. Since a player's arms are attached to his shoulders, it stands to reason that if the shoulders move, the arms also move off the track. And it is also an axiom that anytime the head moves, the shoulders also move. So everything starts with the head. Without a steady head position, it becomes impossible for a player to keep his arms and the putter on line to the hole. He will not secure a square hit and the ball will not roll in a consistent manner. An inconsistent roll, in turn, makes it impossible to judge distance, and the line of the putt will also be lost because of the uncoordinated shoulders. If you watch good putters you will find they keep a steady head on the ball. They hold this position until the ball is well under way. Peeking at the ball generally pulls the putt, because this pulls the left shoulder away from the line of the putt.

The second principle of good putting involves a square contact with the ball. This, too, is a logical statement since we can easily see that if the putter face does not line up at the hole when the ball is struck, the ball will not travel toward the hole. A putter blade facing to the right of the hole will send the ball in that direction. I don't believe everyone must take the putter back the same way, but I do believe that a square hit is always necessary. *Square* means that at impact the putter is aimed at the intended line. The player should evaluate his putting stroke in order to be sure that he achieves square contact.

The last putting essential, tempo, refers to the evenness of the stroke. Fine players always strive for and usually achieve a smoothness in their putting that illustrates this highly important characteristic. A professional player very rarely takes the club back with an exceedingly rapid, jerky stroke and then slows down his stroke on the downswing. He will not do the reverse either. Tempo affects not only direction but the distance of the putt as well. Tempo simply refers to an even stroke; that is, the speed of the backswing is similar to the speed of the downswing. It is this characteristic that makes up the pendulum type of stroke. It is true that some fine putters use a short stroke and a sharp tap of the ball, but they still do not rush at the ball. Their putting strokes are all smooth! In particular, I stress the even tempo, pendulum type stroke because it is simple, easy to learn, and consistent. It is especially suited to older players because it does not require perfect nerve control to operate well. If a player is constantly changing putter head speed, he is very likely to leave one putt far short of the hole and knock the next one 10 feet past the cup. That type of action takes much more control by the nervous system than a more consistent tempo.

Now that we have talked about those factors that are common to nearly all good putters, let us go on to a description of the various strokes in common usage. There are three main varieties of these putting strokes. Each method has its advantages, and each is used by some mighty fine players.

The first method might be called "the dead wrist approach," or the "arm and shoulder stroke." As the names imply, this method involves a stroke without wrist action—in other words, the wrists do not break. The club is swung back with a unified movement of the arms and shoulders and then returned to the ball in the same manner. It is very much like a pendulum motion and generally the putter moves straight back on the backswing and straight forward on the downswing. This is undoubtedly the most consistent of the putting methods because it is the simplest and there is no hinging of the wrists. Shots that involve a great deal of wrist action tend to be more affected by our nervous system. Wrist action can therefore lead to the "yips" and to errant putts, hit with jerky motions and an unevenness of the hands. A golfer who gets the "yips," and starts missing short putts due to jerky motions, usually is collapsing his left wrist and making his putting stroke become flippy. After he misses one short putt, his nervousness increases and he is likely to miss more of them. There is a loss of rhythm that coincides with a loss of confidence. I believe tension will not affect the arm and shoulder stroke as much as the wrist stroke, but on any given day the wrist putter will be more spectacular. Thus the arm stroke is not as spectacular in its results, but it is generally more consistent.

Consistency is the name of the game in golf, especially for older linksmen and particularly with putting. Confidence generally increases as you see that your performance is consistently good; you come to rely upon yourself in that case. I would urge the older player to give the arm stroke a thorough test. If he can use it he will find his touch will improve since there are fewer moving parts. As the older player loses some of the fine control over his nervous system, he needs a technique that is less demanding of such control. The arm stroke is such a technique.

The second putting method does rely on the wrists, and in fact calls for movement of the wrists alone. As the club is swung back, only the wrists move and there is thus a hinge type of action at the wrist joints. Since the arms do not move with this stroke, the club cannot be taken back nor swung through on a low arc. This makes it more difficult to obtain a solid hit at the ball for the simple reason that the club is in a square position for only a brief period of time. Remember, the club is not low as it goes back nor as it moves through the ball; instead, it starts rising so that it is parallel to the ground for only a brief duration. This maximizes the risk of either topping the ball or hitting behind it. Distance becomes more difficult to judge when the club does not make square contact with the ball each time. This is generally a very poor stroke for the older player and there are few players who use it.

There is also another hazard common to wrist putting. It becomes very easy to roll the right wrist over the left, and this cupping action of the left wrist makes it very easy to push or pull putts. These dangers generally are felt to outweigh the advantage of wrist putting—the possibility of sensational control. A wrist putter who is hot has an uncanny touch and will therefore be able to control the roll of the ball so that it gently rolls into the cup. Since only the wrists move, the control of the putter blade can be exceptionally good. But this is true only when things are going well. When there is any tension there is great danger of numerous miscalculations. Tension usually produces the "yips," and then even short putts become very difficult. Since golf is a game that pays off on a consistency basis most players do not remain wrist putters for long. However, as I have said before, if this system works for a player, he should use it with confidence. But if it then begins to fail, he should go to another system.

The third putting method is a combination stroke that involves both wrists and arms. The backswing is made primarily with the wrists, but also involves some arm and shoulder movement. The backswing is low to the ground, but the club does not swing back as low to the ground as is the case with the arm method alone. The downswing consists of a wrist and arm movement to the ball, but there is no cupping of the left wrist at impact. In other words, the left wrist is even with the left arm at impact. There is generally not as much movement through the ball as with the arm stroke. There is a short, firm pop at the ball. While there is wrist break on the backswing, this is not truly a wristy type of stroke. The wrists break on the downswing only to the point where they return to their original position, forming a straight line with the arms. The right wrist does not pass the left wrist.

Arguments about putting strokes have raged for a long time, and they are likely to continue. When someone comes onto the professional tour with a different stroke and is successful, he is likely to be copied. Players seldom stop to consider or ask whether this new method will work for them. While I have no objection to trying out new ideas, I do feel the ultimate test is how it works for you. The same is true with the selection of the putting stroke. I would recommend either the arm and shoulder stroke or the combination stroke. However, if the wrist stroke feels good to you—use it. As we talk about the other parts of the putting stroke keep in mind that these are suggestions too. You might try what I recommend, but always with the idea that you will make modifications if it doesn't feel right to you. With that idea in mind, let us now go to the stance and set-up for putting.

Grip

There are dozens of grip variations seen among great putters, but I will describe my method because I have seen it work well for many golfers. Putting feel generally lies with the right hand. That is the hand that provides the force and therefore gives the most accurate feel for distance. The left hand is the guiding hand and the right provides the power. However, a basic principle is that *both* hands must work together. If one hand predominates, you will either pull or push your putts.

I start, then, by placing all five fingers of the right hand on the club with the palm of the hand pointing toward the target. I next place the left hand on the club with the index finger overlapping the right hand. The back of the left hand approximately faces the target. The pressure points are similar to that for other shots: thumb and index finger of the right hand and the last three fingers of the left hand. Whatever grip you decide to use, be sure the two hands work together as a unit.

The question comes up about how tightly to grip the putter. Some golfers get excellent results by gripping it firmly, while others get equally good results with a very light grip. A student should try both methods and see which provides the best control and feel. Generally, though, either extreme will cause a loss of control. Whichever method he uses, a player should not change his grip at any time during the stroke.

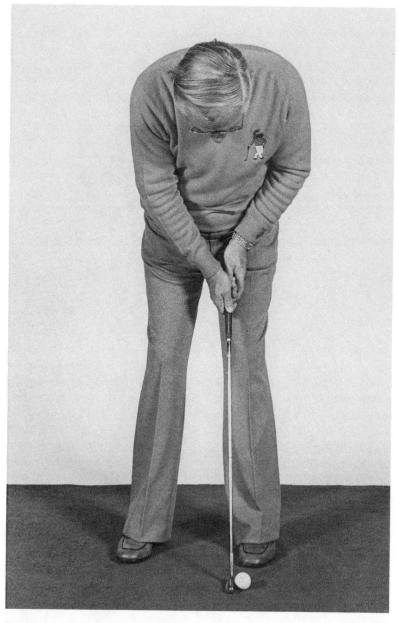

One stroke used in putting. There is no wrist break on either the back-swing or the downstroke. This popular stroke is known for its consistency.

Stance

I recommend a square stance because it makes the stroke less complicated. This merely means that the body is square to the line. Most players bend slightly at the waist so that they are closer to the ball, allowing their elbows to rest on their hips. The exception to this is the very long putt which requires more arm movement. Standing more upright brings the arms away from the body and permits freer movement. Eyes are usually over the ball, giving a clearer view of the line. The ball is placed in the vicinity of the left heel, but there is much variation to this rule. A ball placement more forward near the left foot usually provides a more solid hit since the putter is close to the ground at that point.

Reading the Greens

It is impossible for a golfer to become an accomplished putter until he learns how to read the grain in the greens. This means he must know something about the different kinds of grasses and also note how the greens are cut. A general rule of thumb is that the coarser strains of grass such as Bermuda grow toward moisture and sunlight. The grain, as a result, will run in the growing direction of the grass. Putting down the grain will cause the ball to roll very rapidly, while the opposite is true for putts against the grain. A good method to determine the direction of the grain is to note whether the grass appears shiny (down the grain) or dark (against the grain). A player must also note whether the grain will pull the ball to the right or left.

There are some golf courses where the greens are first cut in one direction, lengthwise for example, then at a right angle to the first cut, say across the width. This generally eliminates the grain effect except near the cup where even slight grain affects the more slowly rolling ball. A player should always note the conditions of the grass near the cup, and the same is true with regard to the slope of the green.

Playing the slope of a green is not something a person learns in a textbook or from another player; only experience can teach him how to do it. Whenever he has a hill to play he must obtain a line and also consider how hard he is going to hit the putt. A slow moving ball always takes more slope. This means that a slope near the cup will affect the ball more than one near the place from which the ball is hit. On short putts, the best rule is to be firm and not play a lot of break. Playing for a sharp break on a short putt will cause the putt to be very

A

The combination stroke includes the backswing (A), during which the wrists are broken, and the downswing (B), a firm stroke during which the wrists return to their original position.

B

During the wrist putting stroke, the wrists take the club back and initiate the hit through the ball.

Because of its inconsistent technique, the wrist putting stroke is not widely used.

weak, and that in turn will allow the ball to be knocked off the intended line by every irregularity in the green.

No one can expect to become an excellent putter overnight. A player needs to develop patience and to learn that no one hits perfect putts all the time. All anyone can do is to get his share of good putts. A golfer who becomes angry at himself because he misses a putt is likely to disturb his rhythm and miss many more.

My advice to any player who wants to putt well is to relax; work on your mental attitude; get set over the ball; and develop a sense of rhythm. As you get older you should be able to increase your control of your thinking. Self-knowledge should add to self-discipline. Since so much of the putting game is mental you can develop that vital link to good scoring. You have the ability to putt well: use it and learn to change negative thoughts into positive ones.

12

Selection and Use of Clubs

Choose your club by assessing your skill and judging the conditions.

At first glance it might appear that in this chapter we can at last get to some guidelines that every golfer can apply. Specific clubs are designed for specific purposes: the driver for teeing off on long holes, the three wood for long approaches to the green, a long iron for slightly shorter approaches to the green, and so on.

Even in this matter of club selection, however, my individual approach to the game of golf is valid. I will talk later in this chapter about how the set-up varies with different clubs, but first I want to cover three important general principles of club selection. The first principle involves playing conditions and takes into consideration desired distance and the variables, such as wind and turf conditions, that affect a player's ability to get the distance needed. The second principle of club selection concerns skill level: after all, there is no percentage in trying to hit a three wood out of the rough if you have trouble getting the ball airborne with such a straight-faced club.

The third principle is the one that I wish to discuss first. It concerns a player's preference of one club over another, and I believe it is generally dictated by something in the player's psychological makeup. Careful mental discipline and an improved technique can somewhat alter this preference. But to make such a change we must take a long look at our thinking and our performance with various clubs.

In all probability every golfer has a favorite club. He will be un-shakeable in his feeling that this club is somehow constructed better than his other clubs. "It swings differently," he will often claim. The same sort of feeling can lead to a special dislike for a club. Many golfers have read the story about how Bob Jones, for example, had one iron he disliked above all others. He claimed that even on his best days he could not get good results from the club. In Bob's case there was a solid reason for this dislike, as things turned out, because years later when measuring devices were developed it was found the club he did not like had a swing weight that was different from that of his other clubs. His marvelous sense of feel had told him that this particular club didn't swing like the other clubs in his set. It would be entirely correct to say, therefore, that he did not have a matched set of clubs. That fault is generally eliminated today by precision matching at the factories where clubs are manufactured. With the current precision matching, for ex-ample, a five-iron and a nine-iron in the same set are made so that they swing alike.

A golfer's own swing error can of course undo what the manufac-turer has built into the club. A certain swing or mental approach can cause one club to produce results that are comparably better or poorer than the results produced with other clubs. In general, if we have confi-dence with a particular club we become more relaxed with it and hit better shots. If we fear the use of a certain club, tension builds up and the swing actually changes. We come right back to the concept of the destructive influence of negative thoughts.

I have seen older players frequently engage in one form of negative thinking. When they pull a long iron out of the bag they believe they must swing harder in order to get the ball airborne. With the short irons they use a smoother swing because they have confidence that the greater loft of the club face will easily get the ball airborne. I have so often heard the comment that older players can't hit long irons because of their loss of strength.

There is also the feeling among many players that when you use a two-iron you must swing harder than with a seven-iron because you want more distance. This kind of thinking, I believe, is the main reason so many older players have trouble with fairway woods, long irons, and, in particular, the driver. When you make alterations in your swing tempo you are destroying the uniformity that the manufacturer built into your clubs. You no longer have a matched set of clubs.

The fact that the shafts of the various clubs in a set are graduated in length means that *the same tempo* will cause the head of a two-iron to move faster than the head of a nine-iron. The longer shaft of the two-iron guarantees this. The player needs to find his normal swing tempo, therefore, and keep it for all clubs. An older player need not make alterations because of his age. The loft on his long irons works the same for him as for anyone else, for example, and will get the ball up in the air. A correct swing will give the club face sufficient speed for the loft to take effect. Even a correct swing that gets the ball in the air might not give an older player as much distance as a younger player might get with the same swing. A player should accept this and strive for consistency. If instead he tries to apply more force, he will be all over the place and his average distance will be *less*. The main thing to work on, then, is thinking.

Each player will have to assess his own level of skill as he reads the remainder of this chapter. I will describe the set-up and technique with the different clubs. But the individual player must analyze his own game in order to determine which clubs his skills allow him to use. Generally, a player who shoots between 90 and 100 will score better if he uses an iron out of the rough rather than a three wood. As his skill increases he may find that he is now able to use a fairway wood even in the rough. But the main point is to go with the clubs that perform consistently well, no matter what they are.

The main change from one club to the next is in the set-up position. Even before we get to that all important set-up, however, something must be said about club selection. Experience will finally pin down how far each player can hit with the various clubs. The beginning golfer needs to strive for consistency by aiming for the same distance every time he uses a particular club, he will be able to pick the right club for each shot.

Now we are ready to talk about that all important set-up. The following material describes the set-up changes needed when going from one class of club to another. (The swing, again, does not vary from one club to the next, so I will concentrate solely on set-up.)

Driver

A key difference between the driver and other clubs is that the ball is played from a teed up position. A player will have to experiment until he finds the correct height to tee up the ball. A general rule would be to have about one-third of the ball protruding above the club face. This will, however, vary according to the type of driver used. With a deep-faced driver (one with a long or deep hitting area between the sole plate and the top of the club), the player generally tees his ball higher off the ground. With a shallow-faced driver, the ball is teed closer to the

There are some golfers who play every shot from the same position, usually well forward in the stance. I don't recommend this because one has to make a very quick move forward with the irons in order to get back to the ball. There is also a tendency to hit the ball too high with the irons. I suggest changing the ball placement with different clubs. With the driver A the ball is played off the arch of the left foot. I suggest placement of the ball just off the left heel B for fairway woods and long irons. With the middle irons the ball is closer to the middle of the stance C and the ball moves to the center of the stance with short irons D. I am using an open stance with all of these shots, but I will accept a square or even closed stance for the long shots if that works best for an individual.

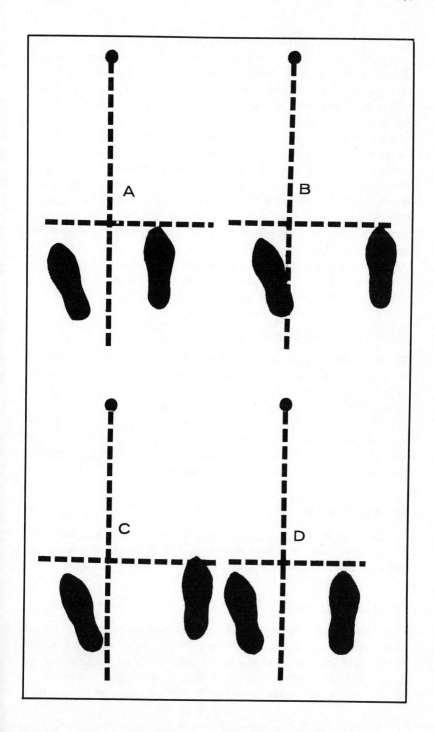

ground. A player must experiment until he finds the best height for his swing and club, and the trajectory off the tee that gives him the greatest consistent accuracy and distance. A very low shot will not carry fairway bunkers, for example, and will cut down distance on wet fairways. Too high a trajectory will cut down driving force, will not carry far, and will die quickly in wind.

Ball placement should be approximately off the left heel. Slightly forward of that position is also allowable if it works, but the ball should *not* be hit off the left toe. That will cause too much of a reaching action and will reduce driving consistency. The width of the driving stance should be the width of the shoulders. That means the outside of the shoulders should equal the distance on the *inside* of the feet. I further suggest an open stance both for driving and for the long irons because this allows the player to move through the ball better. An open stance means that the right toe is about one inch closer to the ball than is the left toe. The remainder of the set-up is the same as what has already been described under the section on basic set-up.

Fairway Woods

The only variation suggested here is to play the ball off the left heel. Or, if that doesn't work, the three and four woods can be played slightly inside the left heel. Inside refers to a point toward the center of the stance. If a player successfully plays all of his woods off the left heel, fine. Generally, however, the older player will have more success with the ball back somewhat on shots other than those hit with the driver. His body simply won't move fast enough to play all shots off the left heel. Stance should be about one inch narrower than with the driver.

Long Irons

Generally speaking, I feel the set-up for the long irons (one, two, three) is the same as for the fairway wood. The ball, again, is just inside of the left heel, but the stance narrowed slightly, perhaps one-half inch.

Middle Irons

The middle irons consist of the four-, five- and six-irons. When we talk about the set-up for the middle irons it also seems opportune to talk about some individual variations. I suggest continual movement of the ball toward the center of the stance along with progressive narrowing of the stance. Yet, there are some fine players who play all of their shots off the left heel. One of the arguments advanced for this position is that a player does not have to make adjustments for each club. As I have mentioned many times, my teaching method does not require everyone to swing exactly alike. If you wish to try this method, go right ahead, and if it works, fine.

I do not advocate it for the average golfer, however. The professional golfer has trained his hands and body to the point where he can consistently make moves that the average golfer cannot make—at least not consistently. And consistency is what makes for lower scores. A ball that is forward in the stance when a short iron (say a nine-iron) is being used means the player must get to the ball faster than he would have to do with a long iron. The reason for this is the point I mentioned earlier about applying the same club face speed to every shot—and a shorter club requires a shorter (or faster) swing. Getting the downswing back into a ball played forward in the stance therefore requires a big move forward with the hips. A man who makes his living at the game can do that, but this is a most difficult move for the average player. It is even more difficult for the older player, because his body generally won't move as rapidly as it once did.

Anyone who wishes to try the ball-off-the-heel method should be ready to give it up if he is consistently missing shots. One variety of missed shot is hitting the ball too high so that it floats toward the target and lacks distance. Another is topping the ball frequently, an error that may be caused by not being able to get back to the ball. Still another, and this is a special problem with the short irons, is pulling shots. The fact that many fine players do move the ball back when playing the short irons proves that the ball-off-the-heel method isn't for everyone. And I believe that moving the ball back as the irons get shorter works for many more players than does the other method.

Consequently, for these middle irons, play the ball about one inch closer to the middle than you did with the long irons. Narrow the stance slightly and use a more open stance. Never overswing with a short iron because here the most important ingredient is accuracy. *If you need more distance simply go to a longer iron.*

Short Irons

Accuracy is absolutely crucial when you select a short iron. Now you are gunning for birdies and you need to be smooth and crisp. That wedge must get close to the pin if you wish to score. Narrow the stance for the last time, play the ball from the middle of the stance, and open your stance to the point where the right foot is now about two inches ahead of the left foot.

The set-up I have suggested will take care of all the swing alterations that are necessary, with no conscious ones needed. That narrowed
and open stance will cause a more upright swing. These two changes will
also shorten your swing to the point where you will come more sharply
down into the ball. The result will be a greater amount of backspin, and
you will therefore be able to hit directly at the pin. Never try to lift the
ball by flipping your right hand at it—this insures a bad shot. As with
any shot, decide what you want to do, set up accordingly, and then let
the club do the work. Trust in your swing and club. Try to get away
from the idea that one club is much more difficult to hit than the
others. Go about it the right way and you will find that all clubs are
about the same.

13

Dealing with Difficult Lies and Trouble Shots

Learn to play out of trouble by knowing your skill level, taking the percentage shots and knowing the clubs.

The average player often becomes very angry when he finds himself facing a difficult lie. This is unfortunate for him because it makes the situation even worse—it tends to cause him to lose his emotional control and this in turn can cause physical and mental errors. Many players do well as long as things are going their way. Let them get a "bad break," however, and a whole round can fall apart. I might add that very often anything other than a level fairway lie is regarded as a bad break.

Playing good golf calls for more discipline than this, and especially by the older player. Furthermore, it's realistic to accept the unfavorable lie as just one more challenge that can be met. The way to meet such a challenge is to learn the various techniques that will be presented here—and thus eliminate any need to worry about not having a level lie. It also helps to remember that even the fairways are frequently not flat; so nobody is cheated if he has to negotiate a hilly lie.

The Uphill Lie

This is the type of shot where the right foot is downhill from the left foot at the address position. That fact immediately raises two danger signals. One is the obvious tendency to sway to the right on the backswing. This "falling down" the hill on the backswing prevents getting back to the ball and usually results either in hooking the ball or in hitting well behind it.

The other problem with this type of stance is getting the weight through the ball. A golfer is literally moving his weight uphill and that requires some adjustments. Still another factor in this shot is that the ball tends to fly higher than normal because the club hits up on it. To compensate for the lost distance this causes, I advise using a longer club than you would have used to get the same distance from a level lie.

This lie requires making some alterations in the standard set-up. The weight goes more on the inside of the right foot than usual; this braces the right foot and helps prevent the player from "falling down the hill." In addition I recommend a slightly open stance to speed up movement through the ball. Also, since it is very difficult to shift the weight completely to the left foot at impact, it is harder to get back to the ball if it's played as far forward as for a normal shot. The ball should therefore be about two inches closer to the middle of the stance than a normal shot would require. Finally, since any time a player has trouble shifting weight to the left foot, at impact he's likely to pull his shot to the left, he should make an allowance by aiming slightly to the right of the target.

I have noticed in my teaching experience that the average player has particular difficulty using the wedge on an uphill lie. It is easy to pop it up much too high, or even to hit behind it. I suggest a more open stance for the wedge than for other clubs when hitting from an uphill lie—this gets the player through the ball more quickly. I might also say that the "punch shot" works very well from the uphill lie. This eliminates the problem of moving through the ball.

The Downhill Lie

Many of the problems faced with this lie are the exact reverse of those faced with the uphill lie. One of the more difficult problems exists when a player needs substantial distance from the downhill lie; and this becomes even more severe if he needs to carry the ball in the air in order to negotiate some hazard. The ball will come off this lie with a much lower trajectory than from a flat lie. It will also run more after it hits because sweeping down at the ball prevents pinching it against the turf. Obtaining backspin is all but impossible. The way to compensate for these tendencies is to select a more lofted club than would be used for the same distance from a level lie.

Starting with the left foot below the right, a condition the downhill lie enforces, makes it more difficult to get the club back; the hips do not move back easily since they as well as the club must move uphill. Sweeping the club back low along the ground will likely ram it into or bounce it off the ground. Compensating for this requires a more upright swing, but does not require any conscious effort to change the swing plane. Here again, the needed change becomes automatic when the player's stance is opened. In order to avoid "falling down the hill' on the downswing, a player puts more weight on his right foot at the beginning and braces his left foot in by bending the left knee in toward the middle of his body more than usual. Finally, the ball should be played farther in his stance—generally three inches back—to compensate for the tendency to hit behind the ball.

The downhill lie requires a special effort, also, to keep the swing smooth. Rushing any shot in golf is bad, but jumping at the ball on a downhill lie causes a player *literally* to fall down the hill and spray the ball aimlessly. Even a well-hit ball from the downhill lie has the tendency to hook, so generally it should be aimed slightly to the right of the target.

Sidehill Lie with Ball Lower Than the Feet

Certainly this is one of the more difficult golf shots. There is a great tendency to fall away from this shot, causing either a slice or a push. The first adjustment involves aiming to the left of the target. Since the ball is farther away from the body than normal, a player must stand closer to it, grip near the end of the handle, and plant his feet firmly. I advise the latter mainly because of the tendency to fall forward on the shot. Since the body does not have a free movement because of the hill, a player should use a longer club than normal and play the ball closer to the middle of his stance than he would with a normal lie.

Sidehill Lie with Ball Above the Feet

The great tendency here is to hook the ball since the swing is much flatter than normal. A number of adjustments are necessary to overcome this problem. The left hand's grip must be especially firm so that the club will not severely roll over at impact. An open stance is needed to make the swing more upright. Aiming right compensates for a hook, and playing the ball well back in the stance (at least to the middle) enables faster movement through the shot. If the body moves past the ball at impact, the hook tendency is sharply decreased. Gripping down shorter on the club brings a player closer to the ball at address. All of these adjustments require using a longer club than would otherwise be necessary.

Experience must be the final teacher in dealing with hilly lies. But there is one guideline that can always help determine where to place the ball in relation to the feet. Stand as though you are hitting the actual shot, but stand in front of the ball. Take a few practice swings and note where the club makes contact with the ground. Then address the ball at a comparable point in relation to your feet when you actually set up to hit your shot.

Play from the Rough

Even the greatest of players sometimes miss the fairway and find themselves in the rough. Obviously, amateur players will encounter this difficulty more often. It behooves us to learn to hit the ball out of the heavy grass.

One thing I have observed over the years is that the average golfer tries to muscle the ball out of the rough. In so doing he attempts to extricate it with his hand muscles. This violates a point I have been making consistently in this book: that a player should never hit as though his hands are doing the job. What he really does is swing the club and let the club hit the ball. Swinging extra hard to "dig" it out with his hands will only cause a player to "cast" at the ball. The right hand will overpower the left hand and the result will be to close the club face. Since the ball won't get airborne quickly it will move only a short distance before the long grass catches and smothers it. I'll come back to the techniques that can get a ball out of deep rough after mentioning a couple of my other observations.

A second major tendency for the high handicapper who's landed in the rough is his desire to make up lost distance with one tremendously long shot. This desire leads him to select a straight-faced club designed for distance. As a result, he never gets the ball airborne, gets it only a short distance, and may still end up buried in the rough. How much better off he would have been had he used a more lofted club and had at least got the ball out of the rough!

Still a third observation involves the lack of recognition by many golfers that a ball sitting up high on the long grass also presents a problem. A ball sitting in this position represents the notorious "flying lie" about which professionals become so concerned. It can't be pinched against solid ground so it flies with little or no backspin when hit. Whereas a player may hit a ball 150 yards with a normal seven-iron he may get 175 yards from a flying lie. The usual preferred solution is to use much less club and to swing very smoothly. If a player is hitting a wedge or short iron, he probably should also open the stance and club face at address, then cut across the ball to give it at least some backspin.

Getting back to the ball that's buried in rough, the first step is to try to figure how much loft will be needed in order to lift the ball into the air quickly. If the ball doesn't rise quickly it will strike the long grass and drop back into the rough. The second step is to use a slightly open stance so that the club will swing back in a more upright fashion to give the ball greater lift. If the grass is particularly long or high behind the ball, the player may have to pick the club up even more sharply on the backswing.

Addressing a ball in deep rough almost always requires an open club face. This performs three necessary functions. It provides quicker lift to the ball. It counteracts the tendency of the grass to grab the club head and force it closed. And it enables the sharper edge of the club to saw through the rough and thus cut down the resistance to the club head. The ball may have to be aimed slightly left of the target. For short shots, the pitching wedge will cut through the rough better than the sand wedge because the latter has a blunt flange. An especially firm left-hand grip is needed in these shots since the rough tends to close the club face.

The various techniques mentioned so far, then, enable a player to deal with hilly lies and shots from the rough, and to overcome the anxiety often related to these shots. And this mental composure further insures success because it enables a player to relax and work on rhythm rather than mistakenly trying to use raw strength.

There are other situations, too, where an individual needs a variety of shots in order to overcome some obstacle. Sometimes these are called "trouble shots," but that term is misleading. Take the high shot, for example. A high shot may be desired from the middle of the fairway in order to take a shortcut to the green. That could hardly be termed a trouble shot. At any rate we talk here about shots that are somewhat on the unusual side and it might not hurt to start with high shots since they are so useful.

Hitting the Ball High

Again, we stress the set-up in order to obtain the desired trajectory. We consciously do very little with the swing itself, because the changed set-up itself alters the swing. The grip remains the same as for a normal shot. So does the position of the arms and shoulders; that is, the arms hang naturally and the shoulders are slightly bent. The width of the stance also remains the same as for a normal shot. A major change is the movement of the ball closer to the left foot, or more forward in the stance. A word of caution should be given: do not place the ball so far forward that it becomes difficult to reach it. If you do, you will find yourself lunging at the ball and in the process flipping your right hand over the left. With that type of action anything can happen, but the most likely result will be topping the ball. This will produce a low shot, just the opposite of what is desired.

Therefore, play the ball comfortably forward. No one can say where to play it in the stance since it varies for each club. Generally you can move the short and middle irons two inches forward of their normal position, and the remainder of the clubs about one inch.

Secondly, be sure that your stance is open. Remember that an open stance causes a more upright swing and this produces a higher trajectory for the ball. You may also wish to open the club face slightly as this provides more loft and will lift the ball faster. There are two problems with this change, however. One is that the ball tends to slide to the right or slice very slightly. The second is that the shot will not carry as far as usual since you have added loft.

As for the swing itself, little needs to be done. I still begin with the weight evenly divided between the feet. Some players start with more weight on the right foot, but the major swing change is to slow down the transfer of weight to the left foot on the downswing. The weight thus stays behind the shot and therefore the club swings more under the ball rather than down into the ball. This catches the ball with an up-swinging rather than a descending blow. As with most other shots be sure the head stays behind the ball. A forward move will cause a lower shot in most cases.

Hitting the Ball Low

As would be expected, the procedure for the low shot is essentially the reverse of the high shot. Yet there are also some very important differences. For example, I do not recommend closing the club face in order to reduce the loft. This is too likely to cause a hook. I do suggest a more nearly square stance and placement of the ball further back in the stance. Except for the woods and long irons, however, the ball should not be placed back of the middle of the stance: among other things it then becomes too easy to push or top the shot. And, it isn't wise to play a driver more than an inch back from center stance because that prevents movement through the shot. Therefore, I suggest an inch back on long irons and woods, and the middle of the stance for the remainder. I also suggest a square stance, or one that is only very slightly open.

One swing adjustment is made for hitting low. The hands are well ahead of the ball at impact. This allows a strong move forward on the downswing and shifts the weight very rapidly to the left foot during the same stage. Then too, of course, it reduces the loft on the club face. Be sure to be extra firm with the left-hand grip because it becomes easy to roll over on this shot and hook it. Also, do not move so far forward on the downswing that you move off the ball. The head can move to the ball, but it must not move *past* the ball.

The Intentional Hook

You may find yourself in the position of having to move around some obstacle. As a general rule, when you have hooked on the first shot, and therefore find yourself to the left of the fairway, you will need to hook again to get to the green. Sometimes you wish a high hook to come over a tree; on other occasions you need a low shot.

The low hook is relatively easy to hit for the simple reason that a hook shot involves a closed club face and that in turn reduces the loft. I suggest a closed club face, a slightly closed stance, and a stronger grip in the right hand than in the left hand. Ball placement is about the same as for a normal type of shot. The backswing is also typical but on the downswing there is a slight rolling action of the wrists with the right hand rolling over the left hand.

The high hook is a more difficult shot to hit for the reasons already stated. This shot will definitely take some practice since it does require more accurate timing and swing precision. Do not close the club face at the set-up position. Play the ball forward and employ a closed stance. Grip the club very firmly with the thumb and index finger of the right hand, and much less firmly with the left hand.

On the backswing take the club somewhat inside, or in a flatter arc. On the downswing roll the wrists at impact and stay well behind your shot. It is important on this shot to avoid any quick transfer of weight to the left leg. If the hips get ahead of the hands you will not be able to roll the wrists over at impact. You will have moved through your shot to the point where you have "blocked out" your hands and that will make a hook nearly impossible.

The Intentional Slice

A slice is a shot that travels left to right because it involves a right to left cutting action on the ball. The club remains open as it slices across the ball, causing a spin that produces the curved flight. This means the club must travel from the outside on the backswing to the inside on the downswing. *Outside* means out away from the body while *inside* means in toward the body.

Direction of movement of the club face alone will not cause a slice because a club face that closes or rolls over at impact will still produce a pull hook. This is a shot that starts left and then hooks farther left. In order to be successful we must alter that set-up position. One very important factor is the grip since we never want to have the club face roll over at impact. It is highly important therefore to have a very firm left-hand grip, and a grip less firm than normal with the right hand. Be especially certain that you have a firm grip with the last three fingers of the left hand.

In addition, use a very open stance. This will restrict the turning motion of the hips on the backswing and tend to cause the club to move outside on the backswing. Open the club face *slightly*: if you open it too much, the ball will simply go higher and not any farther right.

On the backswing, force the club outside the line of the normal backswing and on the downswing bring the club in across the ball and toward the body. This results in a swing type of action, or the outside-in swing that causes a slice. Generally the ball will fly higher with a slice than for a straight ball, and much higher than when the ball hooks.

A low slice is more difficult to achieve. It requires playing the ball farther back in the stance than normal and also a more rapid forward movement than normal. It is an ugly looking swing, involving a lunging type of action, but there it is. In this slice and all other intentionally sliced shots, the club face should be kept from rolling over at impact.

An additional word is in order regarding club selection with intentionally curved shots. Hooking a ball requires the club face to grab hold of the ball and impart spin. It is easier to do this with a more lofted club. With a slice, the ball must slide off the club face, and therefore a less lofted club works better.

The Punch Shot

With most of the shots in golf, a player finishes high. This means that the club is well up over the head and shoulders at the completion of the swing. The hips and shoulders have turned around through the shot and nearly face the target. It might be said that the club has been swung all the way through to the finish of the swing, and generally the full loft of the club is used.

There are times, however, when the player does not wish to use the full hitting effect of a club. He doesn't want as much loft or all the distance the club can produce. He doesn't want the loft or distance of a full seven-iron, for example, but a six-iron would be much too long even though it would fly lower than the seven. Consequently, the player decides to hit a "punch shot" with the seven-iron. He does this in the following manner: he narrows his stance, grips down on the handle (closer to the shaft), stands closer to the ball, and plays the ball back closer to the middle of his stance with short irons—and about two inches even farther back with the long irons. The grip with the left hand is firm so that the club will not roll over at impact and cause a hook.

The backswing is much shorter than for a full type of shot. The major swing difference, however, relates to downswing. Instead of staying behind the ball, the body and head are moved *to* the ball. (Moving the head *past* the ball is bad and causes a multitude of errors.) The club head is swung in such a manner that nearly all of the hit goes into the ball. A sharply descending blow takes place with very little follow-through; nearly all of the impact goes into the ball and into the ground just in front of the ball. Such a blow reduces club loft at impact since the club is moving down, not up, when the ball is contacted. The result is a lower trajectory shot and the ball will run some after it hits. The reduced swing also results in a slightly shorter travelling shot.

There are several important points that have to be made about trouble shots, difficult lies, and general strategy of play. First of all, it is helpful to realize that age is not going to be a handicap as far as these shots are concerned. I will accept the statement that strength can be an asset in getting the ball out of the rough. However, if you use the technique I have outlined you will find the ball comes out of the rough easily and without the use of raw power. The other shots mentioned here do not require strength; only technique.

More so than most components of golf, therefore, difficult lies and trouble shots require a player to develop the mental side of his game. This means that among other things he should take a long hard look at his skills. He shouldn't overplan a round or overthink a shot. The main point here is to attempt only those shots that are likely to come off successfully. Always go with the percentage shot.

The following is an illustration of my point. Let us suppose that you have hooked your tee shot into the rough behind some trees. You note that if you can hit an intentional hook you can curve the ball around those trees and still gain yardage toward the green. Fine, but what happens if the shot does not come off? What if, instead of a hook, you hit the ball dead straight? Now the chances are you will hit it across the fairway and into trouble on the right side of the hole. There, you will likely be in much more serious trouble—and rather than losing one shot you may lose two or three. Remember you can simply chip the ball back into the fairway and thereby set up an easy third shot. With great frequency I have seen players try to play out of trouble only to get into more severe difficulties.

I am not saying that I am opposed to trouble shots. If that had been the case I would not have explained how to execute these shots. Neither am I saying that trouble shots are easy for any player, young or old, to execute. The vital consideration is a player's degree of proficiency with these shots. I do not advise anyone to try shots that have little chance of success and that may well get a player into deeper trouble if he fails. Always go with the percentages, and be sure you know your skill level with different shots. As an older player you can use your wisdom and select shots that you can generally make. Younger players frequently try to pull off the spectacular and in so doing, fail to correctly calculate their skills.

I feel the same way about playing strategy, or what is often called "golf course management." Suppose, for example, that the hole is on the left side of the green. Other factors being equal, the professional favors the right side of the fairway with his tee shot. That is fine for him because he has the shots to accomplish it. But the amateur is apt to drive the ball out of play if he narrows down his target too much. After all, even in this example, a drive to the left of the fairway can still be followed up by an approach shot to the center of the green.

My point is, play to your own game. Don't overtax your abilities. Your main goal is to make solid contact with the ball, and you can't do that if you have placed too many demands upon yourself. It is important to know your own game, and only a player with mental discipline can do that. Age can be a positive factor *if* it adds this special kind of inner control.

14

How to Get Your
Body in Shape for Golf

*Keep your golf swing fluid, with
exercises that limber, relax and
stretch.*

In many respects this is a difficult chapter to present. I have not been a
person who generally requires physical conditioning in order to stay
limber and retain the degree of strength required by the game of golf. I
have found that for me, the best conditioning for golf is golf itself. I
find that I can quickly get into shape with a few rounds of golf, even
after a lengthy layoff.

I do realize, however, that I am somewhat of an exception in this
regard. Most people need some regular program in order to stay in
shape. We have all heard the hackneyed tale of the businessman who sits
around all week and then plays seventy-two holes on the weekend.
Doctors warn against this practice because the individual is not accus-
tomed to such massive activity. As a golf teacher I have some question
about this practice too. After all, no one plays his best golf when he's
tired, and bad habits are likely to be developed.

There undoubtedly are many persons, therefore, who can profit
from a conditioning program, but I want to leave such a program op-
tional. If a person finds himself tired during a round of golf, he probably should work to get himself in better shape. The same would be true
for those persons who have joint stiffness.

However, before we take a look at some possible conditioning programs it seems essential to say a few things about what we want to

avoid. Golf is not a game that requires agility and flexibility, nor great strength. Therefore, I don't recommend any program that might lead to the development of such heavy muscles that movement is restricted. This would be particularly true of the chest and upper arm muscles where a thick and tight muscle structure may well reduce smooth rotation of the shoulders. There also seems another potential handicap of over development of the muscles, and that is psychological. A person who spends considerable time working to become superstrong may become so power-oriented that he tries to muscle the ball. That can only harm the person's golf game.

It seems to me that there are two primary conditioning goals that ought to be achieved in order to improve golfing ability. One has to do with building stamina. Nobody wants to be tired after nine holes of golf. The other relates specifically to leg stamina, because frequently when fatigue does set in we feel it in the legs. Since leg action is so important to the golf game, we must guard against this. Tired legs simply will not be able to move properly through the ball and thereby generate club head speed. Some players use the electric golf carts when they play and this may save some leg fatigue. However, you still need to use the legs when you swing, and if a player isn't in shape he may still be fatigued.

I do wish that every golfer would use the warm up sessions that I suggest in this chapter. Not only will that increase stamina but it will help keep the joints limber. It also helps avoid injury because you don't start a round cold. On the practice range you can gradually ease into a full swing.

Overall, I feel that walking is one of the best exercise programs that exists. This is particularly true for older people who are not used to large doses of strenuous exercise. There are also many people today who enjoy jogging, but recently a number of articles have appeared suggesting dangers in that activity. I have recently noted one word of caution concerning jogging that seems very pertinent for the golfer. Be sure that you do not damage joints by jogging on hard surfaces. I leave it to the individual to decide for himself what form of exercise he needs and can accomplish. Obviously a doctor needs to be involved before any older person begins a *strenuous* program.

Riding a bicycle is a good warm-up exercise for golf.

Deep knee bends help to limber leg muscles for the game.

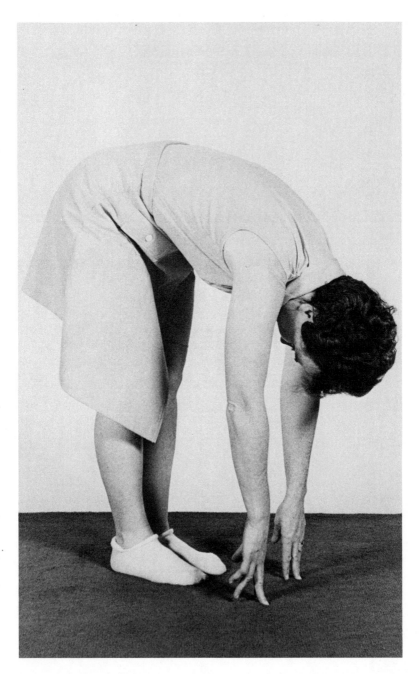

Bending from the waist.

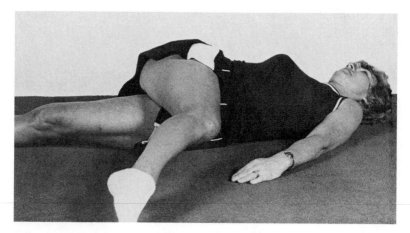

Lying on back, twisting the lower torso.

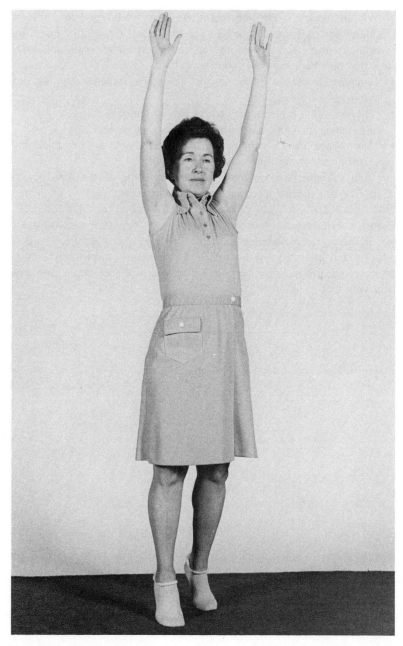

Standing and stretching on your toes is a good way to prepare your body for 18 holes of golf.

We all recognize that with age there is apt to be some loss of joint flexibility and this loss can be harmful to the golf swing. Stiff joints are more injury-prone too. Therefore, let me suggest a few very simple exercises that may help keep that golf swing fluid.

- Walking would be high on my list since it helps maintain leg strength and flexibility.
- Bicycle riding is recommended for similar reasons.
- Stretching, bending and twisting exercises are helpful.
- Deep knee bends, bending at the waist, lying on the back and twisting the lower torso also are beneficial.

Any exercise program that involves stretching of the limbs is advised. Try to establish a regular session, perhaps three or four of them a week, but work into your program gradually and try to make it regular. Even on that first tee you can swing the club easily at first and use a few limbering up movements. Gradually bending at the waist can help in relaxing and stretching taut muscles. Always work toward that which produces flexibility. You may find that you will feel better and also help your golf game.

15

Purchasing Equipment

Match your equipment with your swing, physique — and pocketbook.

Advice on selection of golf equipment is always a very delicate subject. This is true because players have strong preferences that are highly influenced by psychological factors. In my many years of teaching experience I have found that people come to me with two contrary approaches. On the one hand there is the individual who wants the professional to make the complete choice for him. He has few prior ideas about the type of club, let us say, that will suit him best. In the second case there is the person who comes already strongly inclined toward some particular brand of club.

Both instances provide a real challenge to the teaching professional. Selection of golf clubs is heavily based upon psychological preferences, and this is not an invalid basis for selection. However, it should not be the only criterion for selection. There are differences of golf swings and physiques and these differences dictate a particular type of equipment. In other words, clubs should be selected on the basis not only of swing style but also on the basis of psychological preference.

Two points need to be covered about general club selection. The first concerns the price of the equipment. Selection of clubs merely because they are expensive can be a serious mistake that wastes money and fails to aid in the improvement of the golf game. Along this line I have seen many beginning golfers pay out hefty prices for equipment only to find that their game did not develop rapidly. They then become very discouraged because they feel they wasted their money, and their interest in the game wanes. Highly expensive clubs are mainly suited to players who have developed considerable skill. Price of clubs should be dictated by what you can reasonably afford and by what feels good to you.

Secondly, I have heard the fallacious concept that older players need heavy clubs because the added weight will provide force in striking the ball. I have seen some older players use clubs heavier than they should because they felt this proved they had not suffered diminishment of their physical strength. Unfortunately three things usually happen as a result of using clubs that are extra heavy, and all three are bad. The player loses distance; he loses accuracy, and he becomes very tired near the end of his round. What is needed is club head speed and an excessively heavy club reduces this desired speed.

The most important and first consideration in the proper selection of clubs should be the shaft. It is, after all, the shaft that provides the whip type of action needed to supply the force to strike the ball. Consequently it is of the utmost importance that a player select a shaft that fits his type of swing and physique. The average wood is 43 inches long. Each iron is gradually shortened in length from the two iron, which averages 38½ inches in length. If a player is considerably taller than average he will need longer clubs, while shorter players need the opposite. Obviously a club that is too long or too short for the player will throw his whole swing out of kilter.

The flex of the shaft should be determined by the type of swing the player has. If his swing is a fast, strong type the shaft should be stiff or extra stiff. This is recommended since the player is able to whip the club through the shot. If on the other hand the swing is slow, he needs a regular or flexible shaft. The more whippy shaft will help make up for what is not provided by the player's swing itself. The purpose is to blend the shaft with the swing speed physically provided by the player.

A person ought to develop enough psychological maturity not to suffer loss of self-esteem because he uses the flex of the shaft to pick up club head speed. As a player becomes older he is going to swing slower. I can't pick a particular age when this happens, because it is variable from one person to another. I will say that I would be surprised if there isn't some noticeable slowing by around age 60. When the swing slows appreciably the player might consider women's shafts. He will find that the extra whip provided by these shafts will allow him to hit the ball much farther. The rub is that he will also find it more difficult to control the direction of the ball. The trick is to get the blend between player and shaft that gives maximum distance and accuracy.

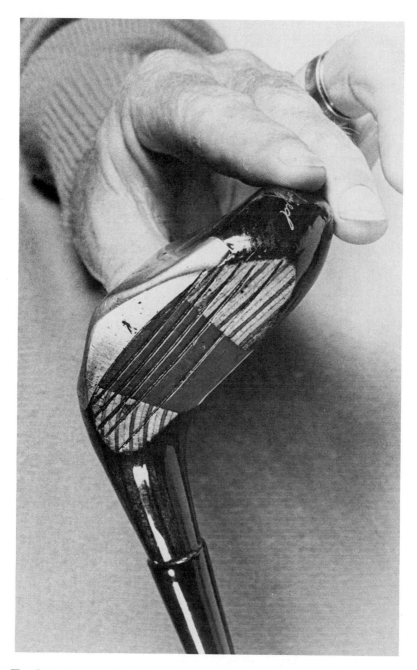

The Ginty is becoming a popular club for older players.

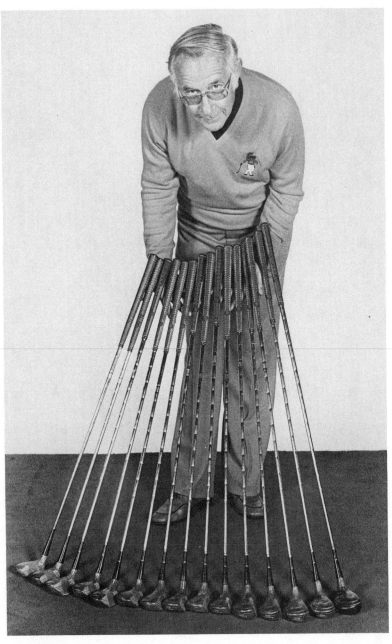

For golfers who dislike iron clubs, there is a full selection of wooden clubs available to choose from.

The graphite shaft has become popular of late and I feel that it makes an excellent club. Since it is a lighter shaft it allows more club head weight while still maintaining the same overall club weight. It can provide excellent results, but normally requires the addition of some weight to the club head. This means that this kind of club can't simply be taken out on the course and good results obtained immediately. A player must take it to the practice range and hit a number of balls, gradually adding head weight until he obtains the desired head feel. If he is not the sort of player who spends some time working on his game, he won't enjoy the graphite shaft. I have often suggested to players that they hit as many as 20 shots *before* adding on even a two inch piece of lead tape; and 20 more shots before they add to or subtract from *that* head weight. Graphite shafts are expensive and generally more suited to the player who shoots in the 70s. It is foolish for a player to invest much money if he can't take advantage of what he has purchased.

The swing weight of the club is one measurement that tells us something about the overall club weight. I generally recommend that the individual player not be concerned about swing weights but only about how the club feels to him when he swings it. The club manufacturers measure swing weights because it allows them to obtain balance throughout the whole range of clubs. In general, though, if you use a regular shaft your swing weight will fall between D and D3. With a flexible shaft it will fall between C5 and D, and with a stiff shaft between D3 to D6. When you select equipment you will generally find that your club professional will be happy to take a look at your swing with a particular club. His advice coupled with your sense of feel and the result of your shots should be the main factors in club selection.

One other factor is also important, however: the way the equipment looks to you. This is important! If a club does not look good to you it will not allow you to build necessary confidence. The results just won't be there. When it looks good you will find that you expect good results and the success ratio is increased. Psychological confidence in a club isn't the total story by any means, but it is very important.

There is some controversy among golfers in regard to the preference of woods over irons. I have often heard the statement that the older players can't hit long irons well. I do not agree that they *can't,* but I do know that they often *don't.* One reason for this is negative thinking. In order to properly hit an iron shot, a player has to hit *down* on the ball. If he's afraid of the shot, he will usually try to lift the ball and the club face comes up before contact is made. The result will be a very poor shot. Since there is more of a swiping action into the ball with a wooden club, many players find them easier to hit. For some reason a large percent of older players are afraid to hit down on a long iron shot. This will make the wood an easier club to hit than a long iron. Whatever the preference, good results come with confidence. If you prefer a wood to an iron, that's fine: woods are now available with so many degrees of loft that they can be substituted for nearly any iron. I don't recommend them, however, as a replacement for the short irons. There is currently a club called the "Ginty" which has about a five wood loft and a bottom grooved flange that helps in the rough. You might wish to try it if you like wooden clubs better than longer irons.

There are two facets of equipment where I do not have a recommendation. One is in regard to putters. Use anything that looks and feels good to you. Putters of all varieties have been used with great success by different players.

Golf ball selection is also a highly personal matter. I would say that if you do not hit the ball with great force you should stay away from the 100 compression ball. It will feel like a rock to you. You may even want to try the 80 compression ball to see if you do not obtain better feel and distance. An older player generally uses a lower compression ball but there is great divergence among players. If you cut your golf ball frequently you might want to try some of the new variety made of Surlyn. The tough material they are made of makes them more resistant to marring and cutting.

In summary, while I have provided you with guidelines the major decisions must be made according to what feels good to you. Bud Gunn said it at the very beginning, and I've been saying it all along: golf is a very psychological game. Both the game and the equipment must be well matched to each player's characteristics, abilities and preferences.

Index